Knowlton School of Architecture
The Ohio State University

TODD GANNON, SERIES EDITOR

SOURCE BOOKS
IN ARCHITECTURE

5

STEVEN SIMMONS HALL

MIT Undergraduate Residence

Todd Gannon and Michael Denison, Volume Editors

PRINCETON ARCHITECTURAL PRESS, NEW YORK

OTHER SOURCE BOOKS IN ARCHITECTURE:
MORPHOSIS/Diamond Ranch High School
The Light Construction Reader
BERNARD TSCHUMI/Zénith de Rouen
UN STUDIO/Erasmus Bridge

Published by
Princeton Architectural Press
37 East Seventh Street
New York, New York 10003

For a free catalog of books, call 1.800.722.6657.
Visit our web site at www.papress.com.

© 2004 Princeton Architectural Press
All rights reserved
Printed and bound in China
07 06 05 04 5 4 3 2 1 First edition

No part of this book may be used or reproduced in any manner without written permission from the publisher, except in the context of reviews.

Every reasonable attempt has been made to identify owners of copyright. Errors or omissions will be corrected in subsequent editions.

Generous support for this project was provided by the Graham Foundation for Advanced Studies in the Fine Arts.

Editing: Linda Lee
Design: Jan Haux

Special thanks to: Nettie Aljian, Nicola Bednarek, Janet Behning, Megan Carey, Penny (Yuen Pik) Chu, Russell Fernandez, Clare Jacobson, John King, Mark Lamster, Nancy Eklund Later, Katharine Myers, Jane Sheinman, Scott Tennent, Jennifer Thompson, Joseph Weston, and Deb Wood of Princeton Architectural Press —Kevin C. Lippert, publisher

Library of Congress Cataloging-in-Publication Data

Gannon, Todd.
 Steven Holl/Simmons Hall / Todd Gannon, Jeffrey Kipnis, Michael Denison.
     p. cm. — (Source books in architecture ; 5)
  ISBN 1-56898-464-2 (pbk. : alk. paper)
 1. Massachusetts Institute of Technology—Buildings—Design and construction. 2. Simmons Hall (Cambridge, Mass.) 3. Holl, Steven—Interviews. 4. Architects—United States—Interviews. I. Kipnis, Jeffrey. II. Denison, Michael. III. Title. IV. Series.

T171.M49G36 2004
727'.38—dc22
                                                            2003023666

CONTENTS

DATA AND CHRONOLOGY	6
CONVERSATIONS WITH STEVEN HOLL	9
MASTER PLAN	21
FOLDED STREET	35
SPONGE	51
PERFCON	70
STUDENT ROOMS	78
FLOOR PLANS	88
EXECUTION	95
COMPLETED CONSTRUCTION	117
CRITICISM—YEHUDA SAFRAN	159
CREDITS	162
BIBLIOGRAPHY	163
BIOGRAPHIES	164

ACKNOWLEDGMENTS

This book would not have been possible without the architecture of Steven Holl and the photography of Andy Ryan. I thank them, as well as Aislinn Weidele, Irene Vogt, Tim Bade, and Anderson Lee of Steven Holl Architects, for their thoroughgoing commitment to the project. In addition, I thank Teri Weidner and Bill Mitchell at MIT for their assistance in visiting the building.

Robert Livesey, director of the Knowlton School of Architecture, continues to encourage and support the Source Books team in countless ways. As always, the advice of friends and colleagues, including Joe Adamson, George Acock, Mitch Acock, Mike Cadwell, Tracy Gannon, Jackie Gargus, Frank Giorlando, Carolyn Hank, Eric Hofmann, José Oubrerie, Jane Murphy, Ted Musielewicz, Ryan Palider, Andrew Rosenthal, Flavio Riva, Chris Shrodes, Karen Soroca, and Tim Welsh, has been essential. Thanks are also due to the participants of the 1999–2000 Baumer Seminars: Cedric Araica, Hyewon Bae, Bhakti Bania, Daniel Blair, Michael Brendle, Ping Cai, Kathy Collier, David Dorfman, Nayeema Eusuf, Miguel Gonzalez, John Hansen, Roberto Jimenez, Maria Kalinke, Sarah Koon, Taeill Kwoon, Michael Leid, Mike Maistros, Christopher Perdzock, Chetan Potdar, Brent Racer, Kimberly Stargell, Dawn Thornton, Jo Ann Vogel, and Yuehui Xu.

Preliminary research for this book was conducted by Bhakti Bania, Bharat Baste, Rujuta Mody, and Manoj Patel. Laurie Gunzelman and Teresa Ball made substantial contributions throughout production, and Kevin Lippert, Linda Lee, and Jan Haux at Princeton Architectural Press provided thoughtful design and editorial direction. Generous support for the project was provided by the Graham Foundation for Advanced Studies in the Fine Arts and by Acock Associates Architects.

As always, the efforts of Jeffrey Kipnis have been essential to every phase of this book's production, and, of course, special thanks to Nicole Hill, for everything.

SOURCE BOOKS
IN ARCHITECTURE

Following the example of music publication, Source Books in Architecture offers an alternative to the traditional architectural monograph. If one is interested in hearing music, he or she simply purchases the desired recording. If, however, one wishes to study a particular piece in greater depth, it is possible to purchase the score—the written code that more clearly articulates the structure, organization, and creative process that brings the work into being. This series is offered in the same spirit. Each Source Book focuses on a single work by a particular architect or on a special topic in contemporary architecture. The work is documented with sketches, models, renderings, working drawings, and photographs at a level of detail that allows careful and thorough study of the project from its conception to the completion of design and construction.

    The graphic component is accompanied by commentary from the architect and critics that further explores both the technical and cultural content of the work in question.

    Source Books in Architecture was conceived by Jeffrey Kipnis and Robert Livesey and is the product of the Herbert Baumer seminars, a series of interactions between students and seminal practitioners at the Knowlton School of Architecture at The Ohio State University. After a significant amount of research on distinguished architects, students lead a discussion that encourages those architects to reveal their architectural motivations and techniques. The students record and transcribe the meetings, which become the basis for these Source Books.

    The seminars are made possible by a generous bequest from Herbert Herndon Baumer. Educated at the Ecole des Beaux-Arts, Baumer was a professor in the Department of Architecture at OSU from 1922 to 1956. He had a dual career as a distinguished design professor who inspired many students and a noted architect who designed several buildings at OSU and other Ohio colleges.

November 1998

Shortlisted architectural firms are interviewed at MIT. Zoning allows a ten-story brick wall.

Steven Holl Architects (SHA) is commissioned for a new master plan along Vassar Street. Possible locations for future residence hall(s) are to be considered within the master plan.

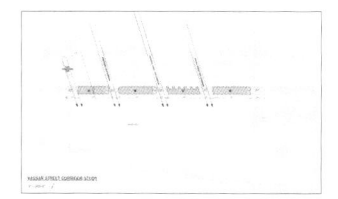

4 February 1999

Preliminary planning studies are presented. The new master plan addressing "porosity" of the urban fabric is submitted with a proposal for four "porous" building schemes. The schemes explore 100'-high "as-of-right" building types as well as 180'-max-height buildings, allowable with a special permit.

28 February 1999

Master plan studies are presented, with two recommended building types, "hybrid tower" and "folded street." The folded street scheme is selected by MIT and SHA for development. Residence hall is set to open fall 2001.

1 June 1999

Complete schematic design for folded street is submitted.

July 1999

Due to possible delays in getting a special-height permit, the folded street scheme is shelved. MIT asks if SHA wanted to develop one of the earlier "as-of-right" schemes, originally presented as part of the master plan, within the tight schedule, which would open the residence hall in fall 2001. SHA holds a blind vote whether to go forward with the project and sacrifice their summer vacations, or turn down the project.

17 August 1999

Complete schematic design for the "sponge" scheme is submitted. Fast track schedule is identified.

6 December 1999

Complete design development for the sponge scheme is submitted.

21 December 1999

A complete concrete bid set, including precast Perfcon panels and foundation package, is issued as an early construction package.

DATA AND CHRONOLOGY

SIMMONS HALL
Cambridge, Massachusetts

Client:

Massachusetts Institute of Technology (MIT)

Data:

350 Student Rooms

Building Size: 53' deep x 385' long x 105' high

5,538 2' x 2' windows

291 precast Perfcon panels were used.

On average, each panel weighed 10,000 pounds including 1,000 pounds of steel reinforcing. The heaviest panel weighed 17,740 pounds.

11 panels were erected per day—one every 35 minutes.

19 June 2000
Construction documents are issued for bid.

Project placed on hold due to frivolous lawsuit from neighbor. The lawsuit delays project for months, missing critical opening schedule of the residence hall.

July 2000
Perfcon mock-up proves that panels can be produced and shipped.

October 2000
Excavation begins.

16 October 2000
Construction documents are reissued.

April 2001
Mock-up room and atrium are completed.

6 November 2001
Topping-out ceremony. Final Perfcon panel is installed.

August 2002
Students move in.

September 2003
Dan Graham sculpture is installed.

CONVERSATIONS WITH STEVEN HOLL

Compiled and edited by Todd Gannon

The following was extracted from a series of exchanges between Steven Holl and the students and faculty of the Knowlton School of Architecture that took place between 1999 and 2003.

ORIGINS

STEVEN HOLL: I was born in Bremerton, Washington, in 1947. The home of the second largest shipyard on the West Coast, Bremerton has a unique industrial landscape shaped by the production of aircraft carriers. It was not surprising to see a three-story building hanging from a crane or massive superstructures hoisted onto ship decks. A strange reality, to be sure, but it seemed perfectly normal when I was young. Of course, there were no architects.

As children, my brother and I built things. Among others, we constructed a three-story treehouse and an underground clubhouse. I have been making things as long as I can remember. The drive to make things—to draw, to sculpt, to build—is something we are born with. There was no clear beginning.

Immediately after high school, I went to architecture school at the University of Washington. There I studied the works of Schinkel, Sullivan, and Wright under Hermann Pundt, an incredible teacher and a great inspiration. At his urging, I spent my junior year in Rome working with another incredible teacher, Astra Zarina, whose insights revealed to me architecture's inseparable intertwining with culture. The trip was a sort of architectural shock therapy. I had never been out of the U.S. before, never even to the East Coast; and I suddenly found myself in a plane flying over the North Pole, traveling from a place of zero architectural significance to one of maximum historical density.

I returned to Washington in 1971 to complete my architectural degree. The Vietnam War was still going on, and late at night we used to watch the televised draft in the studio. I still remember

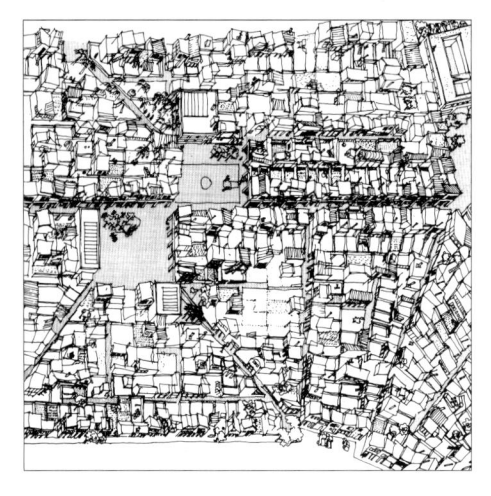

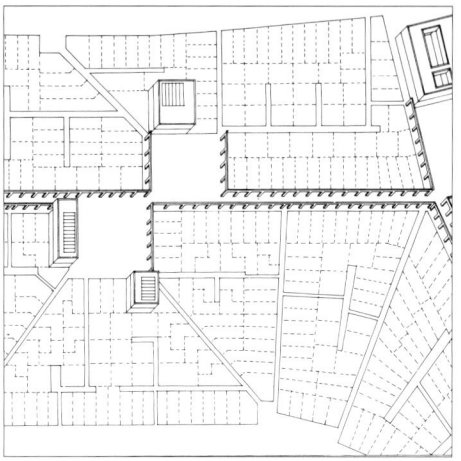

LEFT: Manila Housing, the Philippines, 1975–76, spontaneous house plans
RIGHT: Manila Housing, initial construction

watching those Ping-Pong balls in the basket. Suddenly, there was number forty-seven—I would have to go to Vietnam. I immediately stopped working on my studio project and began my conscientious objection, producing an eighteen-page document outlining my opposition on philosophical rather than religious grounds. My professor was quite progressive and accepted this as my final project, but the local draft board lacked his sensitivity. Bremerton was a military town, after all, and an objection on philosophical grounds was simply not an option. I sent it in five times by registered mail. Finally, I received a reply. "This is the start," I thought. "Here come the court cases." I was not about to go to Canada. Inside I found a 4-F, a release due to physical deformity, and I had never had a physical examination! I was furious. I wanted to tear it up and fight it; I was not about to let them falsify my objection just to get rid of me. My friends convinced me otherwise. "You fool!" they said. "Just take it!"

As a result, I graduated with few drawings. I had spent the last year working on my objection, and had no projects from Rome. I applied to every firm in Seattle but found no one to hire me. Finally, on the basis of my report card alone, I was hired by a small, two-person firm in Bellevue, outside Seattle.

I think the first moments of your education are the most important, just like your first job. It is where you form your value system and build a way of working. But I was in this suburban office doing terrible projects—men's shops and things like that. I did not last there very long. The following year, I went to San Francisco, to begin.

We were going to start our own movement—William Stout, Bill Zimmerman, and myself—we called ourselves "Opus 411." That was the beginning of a pursuit of architecture as a thought process. We would not accept just any internship. Instead, we wrote manifestos, entered competitions. We deliberated on the insignificance of the private house as the only vehicle of private expression. Somehow, architecture had to be more than that. We wanted to explore architecture as more than just an aesthetic undertaking; it had important cultural ramifications.

We explored these ideas in the Manila housing competition in 1975. Our entry was a manifesto against repetitive social housing. Instead of providing an institutional solution to the housing problem, we focused on the psychological dimension of ownership. Our scheme outlined for the residents permanent tenure on the land. Once they owned the land, they would build the houses themselves. Our scheme provided only a street and plaza geometry and a utility infrastructure in the form of arcades. This was no formal exercise, the ideas and attitudes we were dealing with really meant something. Of 450 entries worldwide, I think we placed fourth overall.

After working on a few competitions, I was broke and needed to find a place to work. The most interesting place in San Francisco at the time was the landscape architecture firm of Lawrence Halprin. He was making the most challenging projects, but more importantly, he was thinking. His office respected ideas. We had round table discussions about philosophy over lunch. It was like no other office I'd seen.

In 1976 I went to the East Coast to find a graduate school. I was accepted at Harvard, Princeton, and Yale, but after visiting them I decided not to attend. Instead, I went to the office of Louis Kahn in Philadelphia and asked for a job. I was hired, but while I was back in San Francisco packing for my move, I received word from Philadelphia. Upon his return from Bangladesh, Kahn died at Penn Station. I didn't know what to do. I had declined my acceptance to graduate schools for a job that was no longer possible. At that moment, Alvin Boyarsky, visiting San Francisco, invited me to study, tuition free, at the Architectural Association in London.

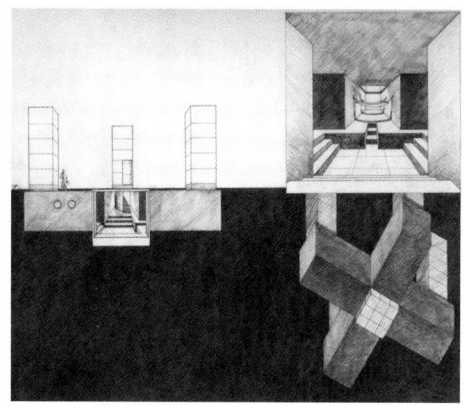

LEFT and RIGHT: Sokolov Retreat, St. Tropez, France, 1976

"It is the place to be," he told me. In another life-changing moment, I packed up and went to London.

Boyarsky was right; the AA in 1976 was incredible. The amount of energy there was unbelievable—there was something like three lectures a day. I tutored in the undergraduate studios with Elia Zenghelis; Rem Koolhaas was presenting Delirious New York as a series of lectures; Zaha Hadid would carry her parallel bar around with her, demanding to be taught how to draw.

While in London, I traveled quite a bit. I went to every possible building to experience them firsthand, to sketch. I lived as a vagabond, a rumpled, dirty figure trying to find a way to do a project.

Somehow, through a friend, I met a man in Paris who was dissatisfied with his vacation house in San Tropez. It was noisy, too crowded; he needed a retreat from the house. I said, "Sure, I'll make you a project."

To allow him to escape from San Tropez, I designed an underwater retreat floating in the bay. It was to be constructed of ferro-concrete—the same thin-shell technology used in naval architecture—and would have a transparent bottom. One would row out to it from the mainland. The deck would float four centimeters below the surface; visitors would remove their shoes and roll up their pants to get to the entry. After descending a central staircase, one would enter an absolutely silent world. Swinging in a hammock, one could look out the portholes at the fish. After being down there a while, one might go a little crazy, so it is possible to climb a ladder and jump from the tower into the sea.

This was 1976, an incredible time for architecture. Everyone was making obsessive drawings. Bernard Tschumi was producing the Manhattan Transcripts, Daniel Libeskind was doing his Chamberworks. I made ten large pencil drawings of the San Tropez project incorporating views that not only reinforced the ideas of the project but also resonated with the way I felt about my working as well. The character in the rowboat illustrates the way that all of us must work. He cannot see where he is going, only where he has been. Progress is tempered by a sense of mystery, of doubt.

TODD GANNON: Another important work from that period was the Gymnasium-Bridge. Tell us about that project.

SH: I made the Gymnasium-Bridge in my brother's painting studio in New York City. The given program was simple: a footbridge spanning the Bronx Kill, connecting the South Bronx to the park on Randall's Island. I proposed something more than just a simple bridge. I conceived of the project as a social condenser, a catalyst for activities generated by the fusion of these two programs. Destitute persons would come to the bridge for a month to work out, to recondition themselves both mentally and physically, and then return to society. While physically bridging the water, it also acted as a conceptual bridge, affecting a transition from one reality to another.

The project takes the form of bridges over bridges, with various programs occupying different zones. Strenuous activities such as boxing, handball, and "long basketball" (an invention of mine generated by the linear form of the bridge), take place along the top of the long span while quiet activities—chess, checkers, billiards—occupy the short span. A section of the largest bridge pivots to allow ships to pass. Water activities are stacked in the smaller bridge: docks, rowing club, steam rooms, showers, ice rink, river observatory. At night, the translucent glass skin glows along the project's axis, lighting the pathway below. The figure in the rowboat appears again, still not knowing where he's going, only where he's been.

Again, this project was made with a series of elaborate pencil drawings. With this method, I had formed a vocabulary of exploration that would persist for the next four years. All the drawings were black and white, all in pencil.

opposite:
Gymnasium-Bridge, South Bronx, New York, 1977

JEFFREY KIPNIS: **These are incredible drawings. There exists an architecture to the black, an exploration of the texture of the paper and of the graphite. These are important explorations in graphic technique.**

SH: Though I no longer make these elaborate pencil drawings, I still maintain that the process of conception in architecture must be an analog one—it must begin with an idea between the hand and the mind. These were demanding drawings; they took forever. It was a wonderful way to work, but rarely do we have time for it. This is why I changed to watercolor. With this medium, I can produce a sketch in thirty minutes instead of three days. With watercolor, I can work quickly to study light from the beginning of the project. These sketches can do more to elucidate the idea and the spaces of a project than a simple diagram ever could.

TG: **The Gymnasium-Bridge won a Progressive Architecture Award in 1978 and became the subject of the first issue of Pamphlet Architecture. Could you tell us about this chain of events?**

SH: That was an exciting moment for me. I remember the feeling—I've made it in New York, now it will all be at my feet. I went to the awards ceremony, prepared for an exciting event, thinking I would meet all these important people. The reality proved otherwise. On one side of our table was an elevator salesman, on the other, a roofing salesman. The event was a real disappointment.

I was also frustrated with the way the work was presented in *Progressive Architecture*, the way all work tends to be presented in magazines, with tiny pictures accompanied by inane text. I wanted to present the work properly, to clearly elucidate the ideas. Bill Stout had opened a little bookstore in San Francisco, so I called and said, "Let's start a publication. We'll just do manifestos and single projects." The first issue was the bridge project. We printed one hundred copies for something like $215.

I was living in New York at the time and had a teaching position at Syracuse. I was a registered architect but could not tolerate working for anyone else. The teaching salary was not enough to live on (it barely covered the air and taxi fare to and from Syracuse) so I was working in the mornings at an engineering firm. I would go in at 8:30 and work until 11:30, then go home and take a nap. I would get up at 1:00 and draw until 1:00 in the morning—a strange existence, very idealistic. Occasionally a client would come along—a small addition in Millville, New Jersey, a loft renovation on Twenty-sixth Street—but mostly I was working on theoretical projects and competitions.

I was very lucky to find incredibly cheap space in which to live and work. It was on Twenty-first Street and the rent—just $275 a month—was not changed for ten years! The view was of the Saphardic Jewish Cemetery. When friends would come to visit from Europe, they could not believe they were in Manhattan, because all you could see was this huge cemetery.

I slept on a plywood shelf above the entrance. There was no hot water, so every day at 6:00 I would go to the YMCA to take a shower. At night, the building was absolutely empty—a wonderful place to work! Having that place for so little money was like a grant. It enabled me to be in New York and work on these projects. Most, like the Bridge of Houses, or Pamphlet Architecture, had no clients. This was okay, because with a very small amount of money I could maintain this bohemian lifestyle.

JK: **Let's talk a bit about your attitude toward the articulation of details. I'll begin with what you have called your first work of architecture, the Pool House and Sculpture Studio in Scarsdale, New York. In this house, there is a descriptive attention to small detail that seems to be receding in your more recent work. You describe an almost fetishistic**

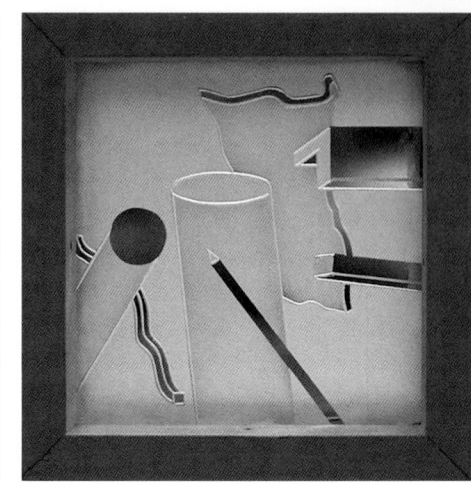

LEFT: Pool House and Sculpture Studio, Scarsdale, New York, 1981, interior view
CENTER and RIGHT: Sandblasted glass details

attention to detail in such items as light fixtures, soap dishes, special windows. These items perform a number of tasks in your projects: they reinforce the architectural ideas, they help the visitor to "get it," and they are also often quite beautiful. Even so, I would argue that there are moments within a project that the architect should simply leave alone, that there is a danger of undermining the architectural intentions through an excess of articulation.

SH: I think the level of articulation depends upon the project. The pavilion in Scarsdale was undertaken with a very free hand. In addition, it is a very small building—only 11 feet wide. The project does not work well as a space; there really is no space there, just a large, blank wall. Given this, the idea that elements at a small scale could operate at a heightened material intensity was intriguing to me. The result was an intensification of certain areas and a stirring blankness in others. Perhaps it was a way to introduce a greater degree of difference into a very small space.

The strategy is similar to that of the Kiasma Museum in Helsinki, where we deliberately tried to eliminate the intermediate scale. In a sense, both projects take up an anti-postmodernist position. For example, a corporate firm like Kohn Pederson Fox works almost entirely at the intermediate scale—think of the plaid patterning in their window mullions. In their work, one finds visual interest in the intermediate zone of the pattern, but an utter lack of attention to the small scale. These patterns turn out to be factory-made extruded aluminum windows, devoid of any attention at a small scale. We work in a manner akin to Pierre Chareau or Carlo Scarpa, with a greater interest in the detail. Scarpa was, in fact, a great inspiration for us. In our eyes, he validated a modest practice. One did not have to build skyscrapers; architecture could be explored in simple structures and small-scale work.

LEFT: Kiasma Museum, Helsinki, Finland, 1993–98, view from the south
RIGHT: Kiasma Museum, view of gallery

JK: **I have a similar reaction to Scarpa's work. When he is willing to leave things alone, as at the Castelvecchio or Querini Stampalia, the work becomes transcendental. But in projects where his hand is evident over every square inch of the work, say at the Brion-Vega cemetery, he introduces a fuzziness that, for me, ruins the work.**

It is important for an architect to decide where to play and where not to play. In Helsinki, for example, the exterior has quite a bit happening in the middle register, akin to the urban noise and visual information found in any city. But inside, you leave out the middle register entirely, giving the silence an almost visceral quality. This transition from the cacophony of the urban milieu to an **interior world of light and emptiness is an incredible choreography of moods.**

SH: But you need space to do that. In Scarsdale, we had no space. You have criticized the chapel of St. Ignatius for this need to touch every square inch. Perhaps that criticism is valid, I don't know.

JK: **When an architect takes a job, someone has put his or her whole world into another's hands. It is incredible, even in something as insignificant as the wall of a pool. I think what often happens is that this responsibility compels architects to affect every inch of the project, to give it everything that they have got. It takes an incredible maturity and courage to know when to leave things alone. Robert Slutzky once told me that the hardest decision an artist has to make is to take out something he likes. I think this is a brilliant statement.**

SH: But this is also very much affected by the times. If, for example, we were to look at the work of Frank Lloyd Wright or Alvar Aalto or Sigurd Lewerentz, we would see in each case an architect who was trying to affect the space down to the last detail. When we did Scarsdale, we were occupying

CONVERSATION 17

a different time, a moment when it seemed that the passion of Aalto or Wright had dissipated in our "great masters." Philip Johnson would put up entire buildings with nothing but off-the-shelf products and fixtures. There were many architects practicing this way. Our work was an effort to say, "Wait a minute, architecture is more than selections from *Sweet's Catalog*!" We wanted to care about the light fixtures, about the furniture we used. I think we shared this notion with others working at that time—Thom Mayne and Michael Rotundi, for instance. Their work exhibited the same obsessive quality.

I can remember the handle on a window at a Wright house in Oklahoma. Ordinarily, the window handle would be a minor experience, something one would not likely notice. But Wright adds a delicacy and grace to the element that makes it memorable. I think that the human experience of architecture is bound up in these sorts of elements. Personally, I do not accept an architectural idea based solely on concepts. There has to be a material component. It is a shame to see a building—and there are some here in Columbus—that has a strong concept but no material component. With interiors composed of sheet rock and acoustical tiles, the experience falls flat.

Materiality has the potential to profoundly affect the experience of space. Take Wright's Hollyhock House, for example. The front door is made of concrete—the heaviest door I have ever pushed. It is a strange and interesting feeling to open this door, one that cannot be captured in a photograph. In a space designed by Wright, I do not notice the intricate patterns in the leaded glass windows. I notice the unbelievable patterns of light cast upon the walls. What a joy to see this light change throughout the day, to witness the house interact with Nature. I am very interested in this type of exploration in architecture.

TG: **It seems that there are two issues at play here. One is the *Gesamtkunstwerk*, or total work of** art. This is the architecture of the Wrightian house, an environment wholly affected and controlled by the hand of the architect. The other issue is the idea of estrangement. The Russian literary critic Viktor Shklovsky invoked the technique as a means to reawaken our senses to the world around us. In his essay "Art as Device," Shklovsky employed the work of Leo Tolstoy to illustrate its use. The technique refreshes the object by making it "strange." I think this is exactly what Wright does with the concrete door at the Hollyhock House. Through a modification of materiality, he intensifies the doorness of the door, making the act of passing through it worth noticing.

SH: Exactly. This is clearly no new idea; one finds it throughout the history of literature. Marcel Proust told us how to have a cup of tea or eat a cookie. He could spend thirty pages on the taste of a madeleine, or on not being able to sleep at night. These works have the ability to reawaken our senses, as you said. After reading these works, or experiencing this type of architecture, your senses are more cognizant, you see things differently. One of the urgent missions for architects and city planners today is this task of awakening the senses. As architects and planners, one of the most important things we can do is to rekindle a psychological realization of space in people. These things we are talking about now are ways to do this. It does not mean that every moment in a project has to be expensive or hyperarticulated.

MASTER PLAN

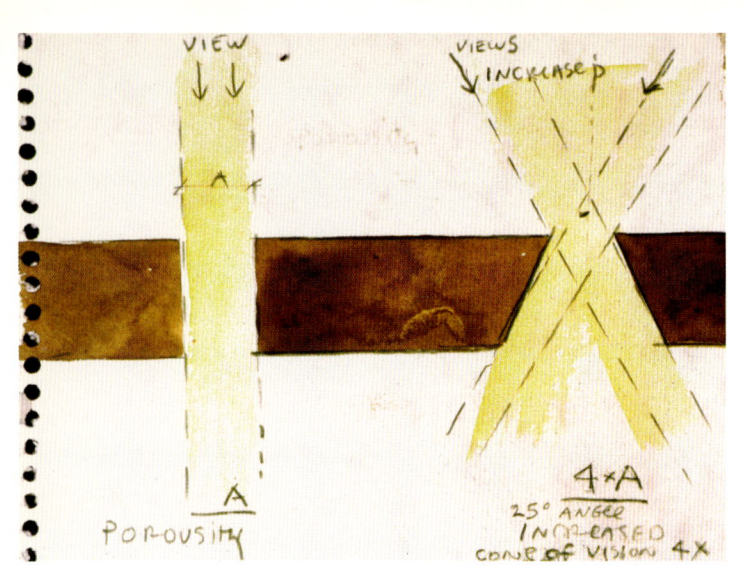

Porosity diagram

opposite:
Houses of Individuation, concept sketch

Instead of a homogenous brick urban wall we envision the new residential strip as a porous membrane made up of four or five experimental individual buildings. Each of the residences would be a unique "house" with a particular identity. The visual space, light, materiality, transparency of these buildings are particularly important as they have a position free of the normal city fabric on both sides. In a sense they form a "facade" for the residential district to be built to the north of them. As a facade they must attempt to not block views. They should be "permeable." The urban planning of the residential dormitories should support their maximum potential as inspirational places to live and study.

QUALITIES

porous, permeable
riddle, sponge
sieve-like, sieve
honeycomb
cribiformity
screen, net

opening, hole
aperature, passageway
pervious, unrestricted

BUILDING TYPES AND PERMEABILITY

vertically permeable
horizontally permeable
diagonally permeable (plan)
diagonally permeable (section)

22   MASTER PLAN

"SOCIAL CONDENSERS"

The dormitory residence as a special housing type is not quite transient and not quite permanent. Social spaces must be planned to bring people together, provoking interaction, friendship, dialogue, etc. The permeable openings would correspond to meeting places, terraces, lounges, and activated passageways. Porosity as a massing concept would have programmatic potentials.

HOUSE OF INDIVIDUATION

Individuation in housing is a modern aim for invigorating aggregate housing of all types. In the case of a residence hall, individuation of the student's room, individual character of the cluster or collective portion, and individuation of the overall residential buildings can contribute to the vitality and identity of the residents.

While the collective areas aim to provoke interaction and exchange, individual souls are given consideration over mass population.

—Steven Holl, *from 1998 master plan text*

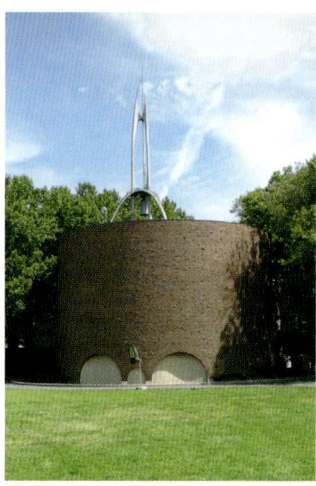

LEFT: Alvar Aalto, Baker House, Cambridge, MA, 1947–49, exterior view
CENTER: Eero Saarinen, Kresge Chapel, Cambridge, MA, 1955
RIGHT: Eero Saarinen, Kresge Auditorium, Cambridge, MA, 1955

opposite:
MIT campus, aerial view

MASTER PLAN

TG: How did the Simmons Hall project begin?

SH: Simmons Hall is one component of a much larger building program undertaken by the Massachusetts Institute of Technology. Frank Gehry is involved with the Stata Center, Kevin Roche's athletic facility was underway when we began, and a media lab by Fumihiko Maki will begin soon. With these buildings, MIT wanted to start with a clean slate. They wanted to forget about the mediocre buildings that have been built there over the last fifteen years and instead look back to the impressive work of Alvar Aalto and Eero Saarinen as models of excellence to which a new generation of architects would rise.

We had our first interview in November of 1998. A master plan had been completed which called for a series of very normative, pseudo-traditional buildings along Vassar Street. If implemented, the plan would result in a five- or six-story brick wall along the entire length of Vassar Street, essentially blocking the neighborhood of Cambridgeport to the north from Briggs Field and the river.

At the interview, I explained that we would be thrilled to work at MIT, but in order to do so, we would reject the master plan. Aside from its lack of consideration for its neighbors, the plan, with its call for traditional buildings and normative streetscapes, was, in our opinion, too concerned with the past. MIT is an incredible research institution, a place concerned with advancing knowledge for the sake of a better future. Why should its architecture aspire to the past? The best architecture on campus, Saarinen's Kresge Auditorium and Chapel, Aalto's Baker House, does not do this. Instead, these works celebrate the possibilities of the future. In the same spirit, we were determined to make a project that was unashamed to be part of the twenty-first century.

opposite:
Simmons Hall, site plan

We proposed to develop a new master plan that would address the shortcomings we saw in the existing plan. Larry Bacow, MIT's chancellor and leader of the campus-building program, was a great risk-taker. He said, "Okay, do it."

For six weeks, we devised methods for dealing with this difficult site. Vassar Street, formerly an industrial artery with a few imposing brick warehouses still present, is 55 feet wide and over 2,100 feet long. To the north, railroad tracks run parallel with the street, and the residential neighborhood of Cambridgeport lies beyond. To the south are Briggs Field, Aalto's Baker House, and the Charles River. We felt that it was imperative to maintain a connection with the neighborhood beyond, and very soon we began thinking of ways to maintain a sense of openness.

Porosity became the theme; the absence of building would be the object of the plan. To accomplish this, we devised a diaphanous edge of dormitory buildings, with pocket parks aligned with the existing streets to maintain view corridors. Each building would be exactly 25 percent porous, with one quarter of its mass missing, maintaining a connection to the neighborhood beyond.

The view corridors defined four building sites. On each site, we developed different manifestations of porosity. These different notions—vertical porosity, horizontal porosity, diagonal porosity, and so on—soon gelled into distinct building ideas. Among others, there was a scheme of towers, a sponge, a folded street, a dendritic or treelike scheme, a void space scheme, and various hybrids. Each building was quite distinct formally, but they were unified by the theme of porosity.

In tandem with these ideas, we studied the idea of individuation. Each building would accommodate roughly 350 students in about ten distinct "houses," individual communities of thirty to forty students. Rather than conform to the typical dormitory model, which is too often conceived as an undifferentiated filing cabinet for bodies, we

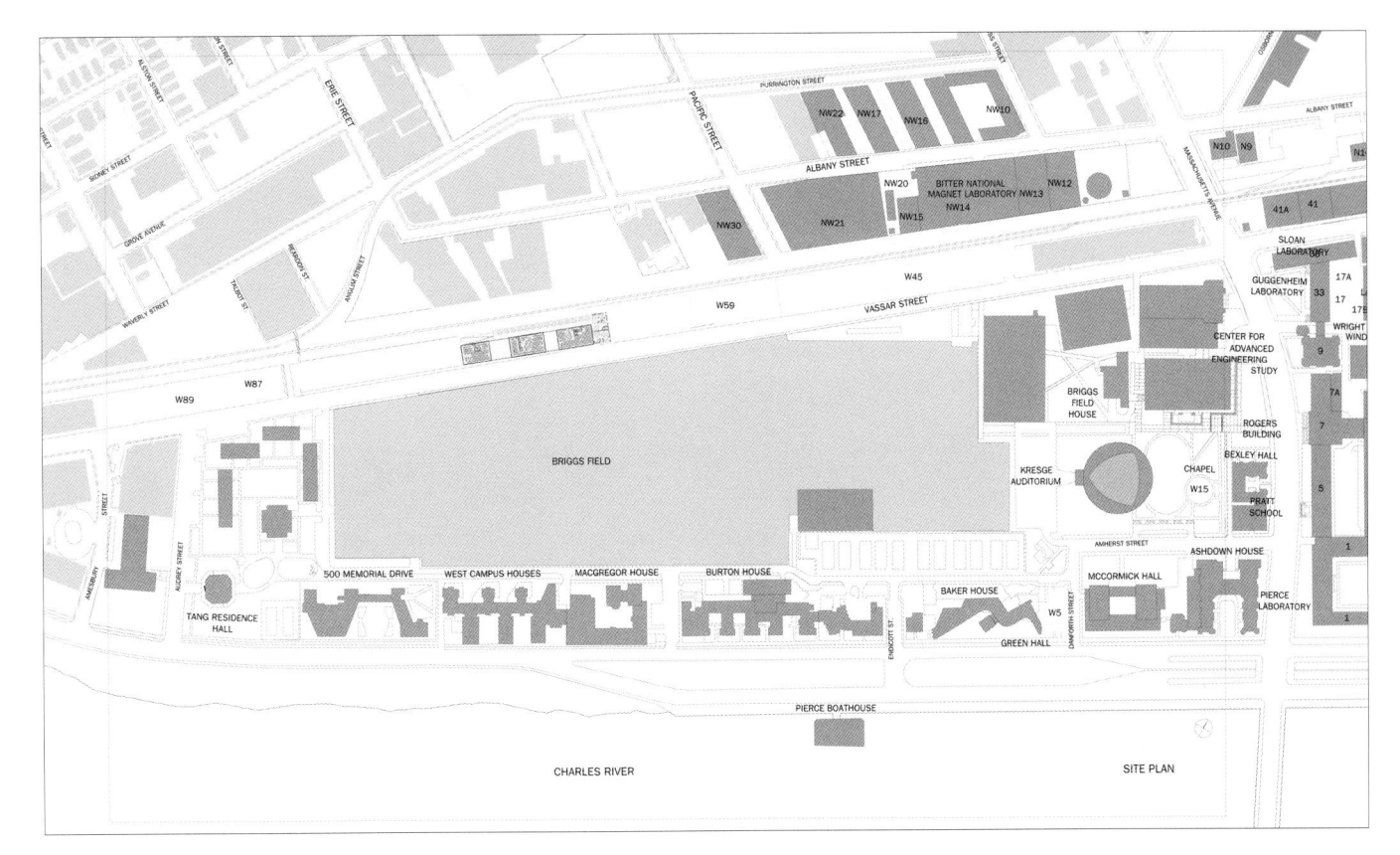

SITE CONSIDERATIONS
Preliminary Planning Strategies

VASSAR STREET CORRIDOR
The site is a very particular and unique strip of land 90' wide and over 2,100' long with a railroad at its north side and athletic fields and distant river views at its south side. In 1903 Cambridge planned to divide the site with four streets—Erie, Wolcott, Robinson, and Greenhage—to physically connect the neighborhood with the river. The current Vassar Street Corridor Master Planning process is an opportunity to realize these physical and visual connections through the site in conjunction with the planned residential redevelopment of the surrounding areas. To the north of the Vassar Street Corridor site we would propose to adopt the brick courtyard typology described in the Koetter Kim report.

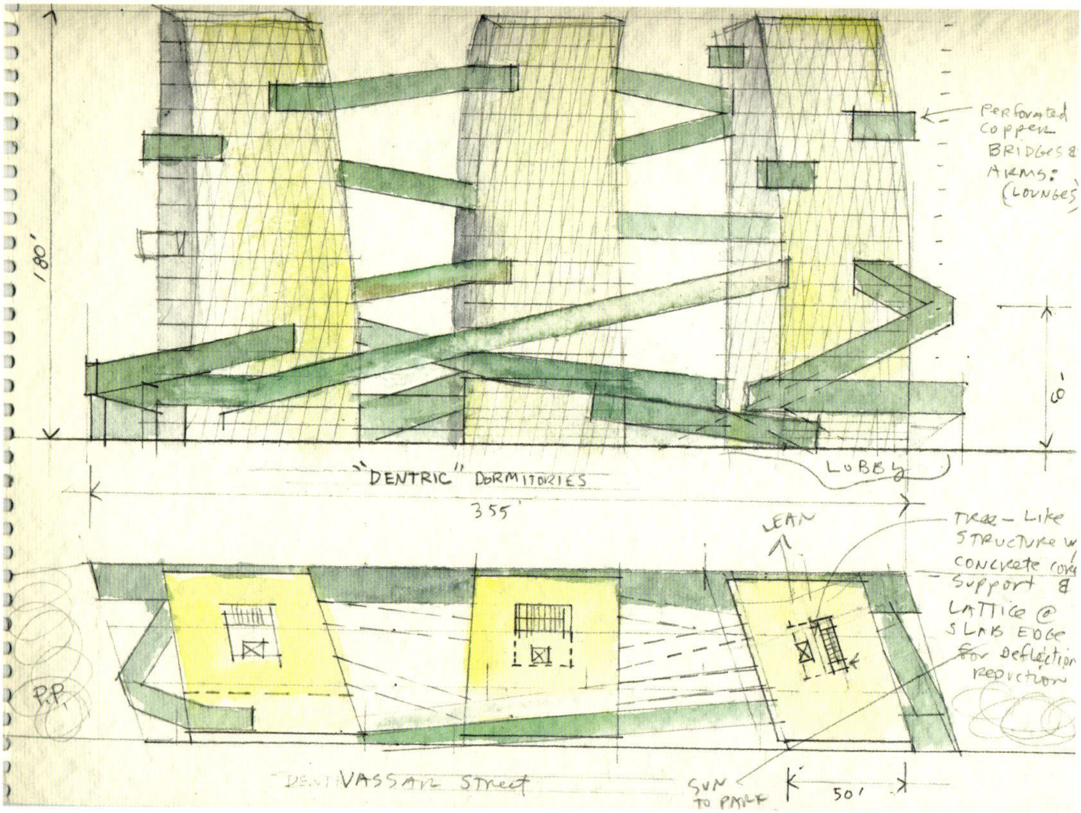
Perforated copper
BRIDGES & ARMS: (LOUNGES)
180'
60'
"DENTRIC" DORMITORIES
LOBBY
355'
LEAN
TREE-LIKE STRUCTURE W/ CONCRETE
SUPPORT &
LATTICE @ SLAB EDGE
for deflection reduction
P.P.
VASSAR Street
SUN TO PARK
50'

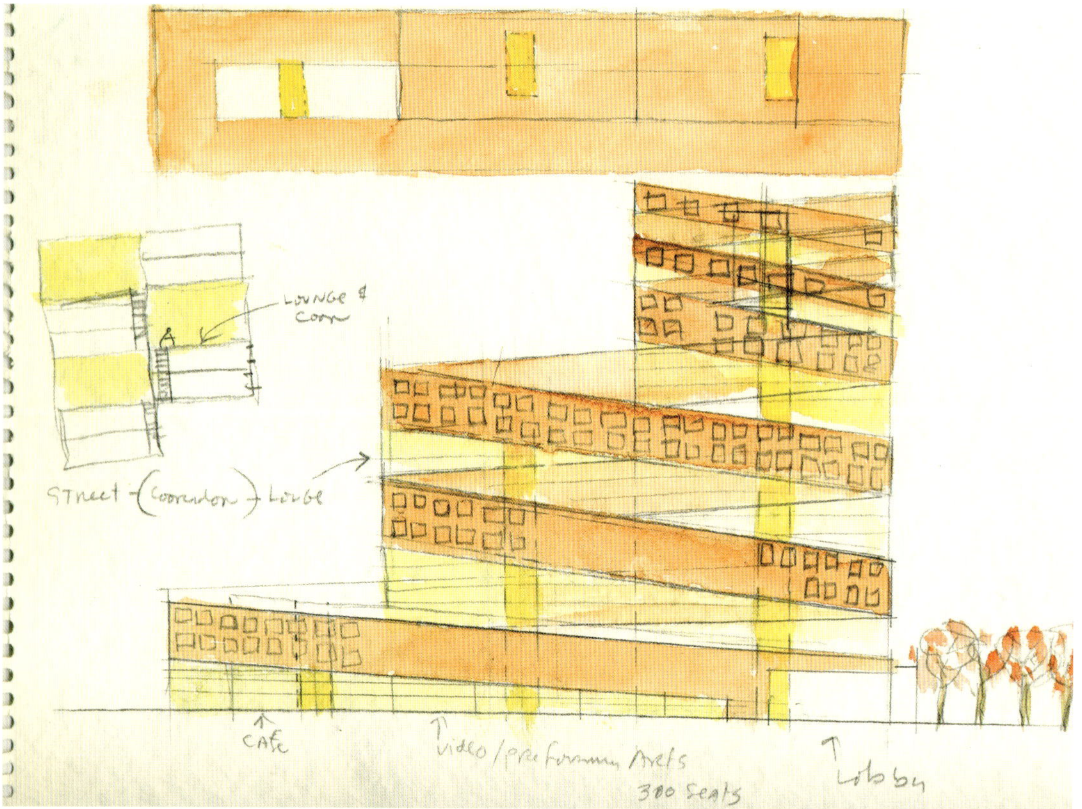
LOUNGE & CORR
Street (corridor)
Cafe
video/performing Arts
300 Seats
Lobby

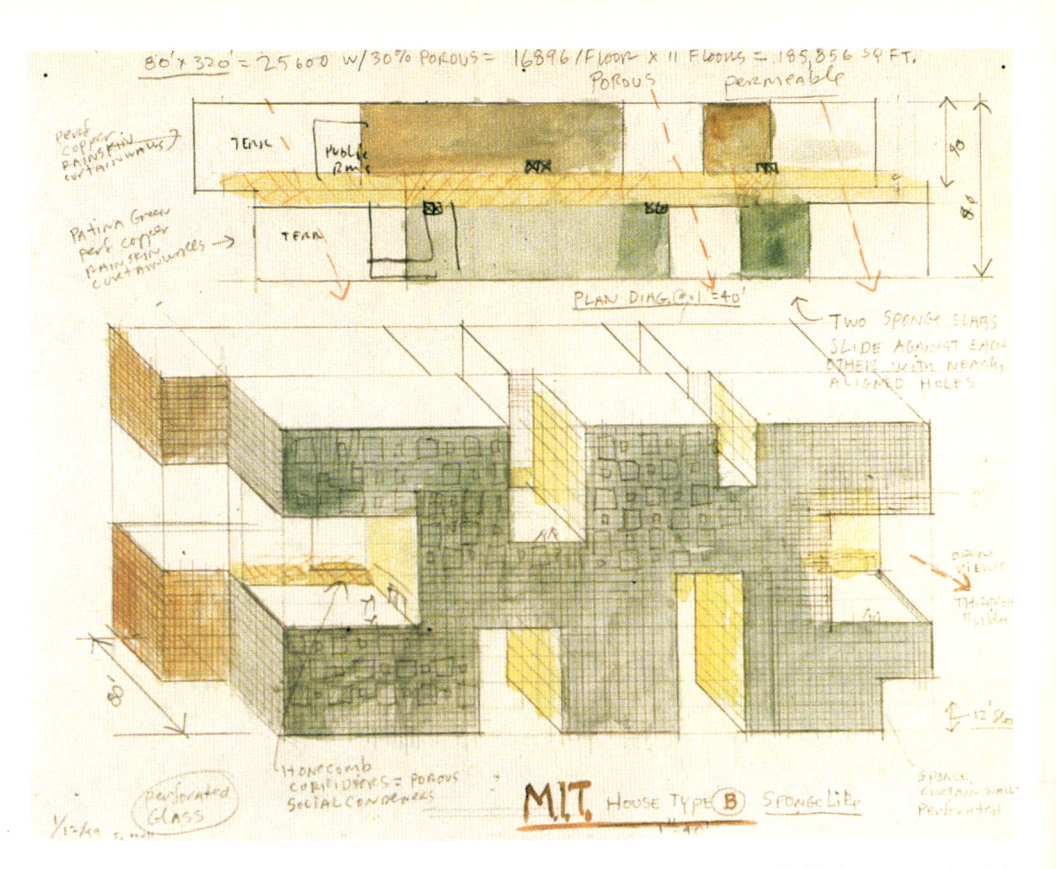

Hybrid scheme, watercolor study

opposite:
TOP: Dentritic scheme, watercolor study
BOTTOM: Folded street scheme, watercolor study

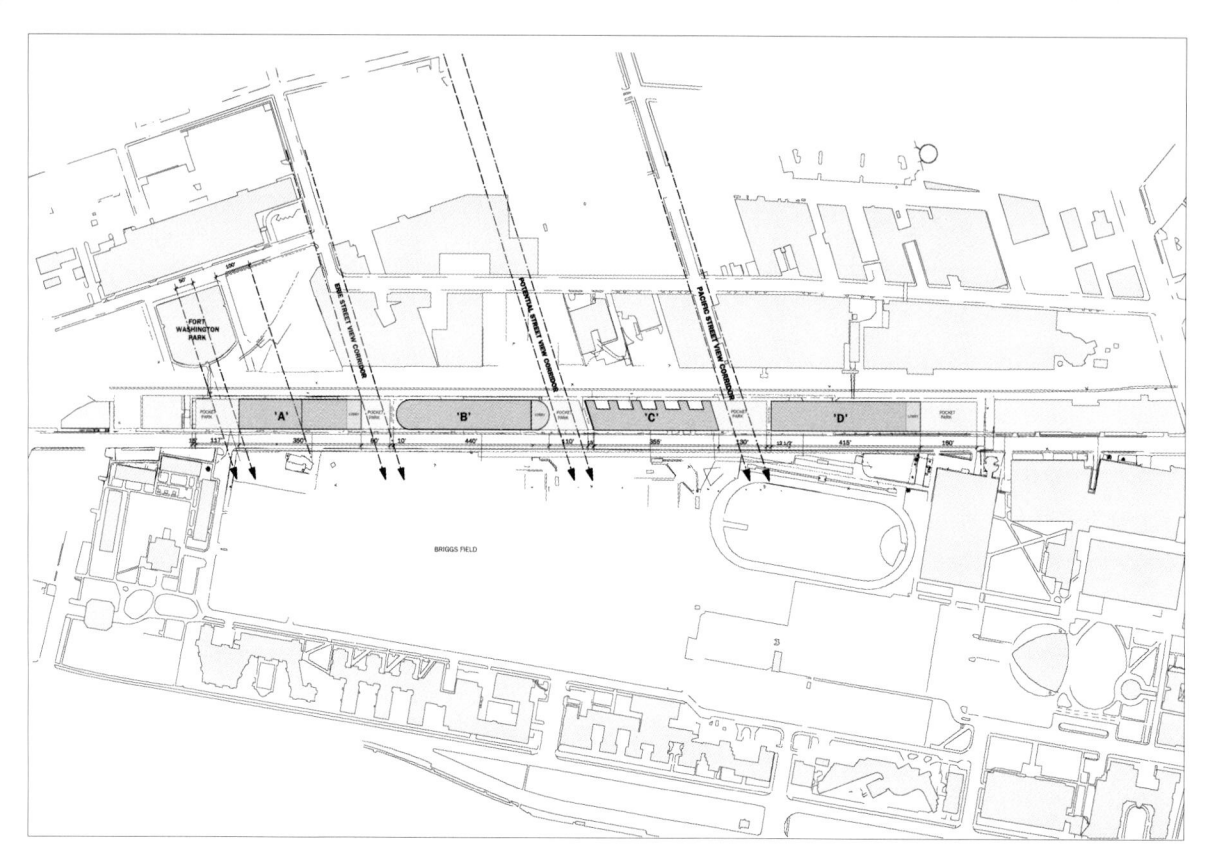

searched for ways to make as diverse a range of spatial experiences as possible. Each building—indeed, even each house within the buildings—would offer a range of spatial qualities, of textures, of colors. Even the pocket parks began to take on individual personalities. We strove to make spaces that would inspire the students who lived there, to compel them to revel in the unexpected, to see the world with fresh eyes.

At the end of six weeks, we had another meeting with Larry Bacow. He was impressed with the work we had done and asked us which building we felt would be most interesting to develop. We chose the folded street.

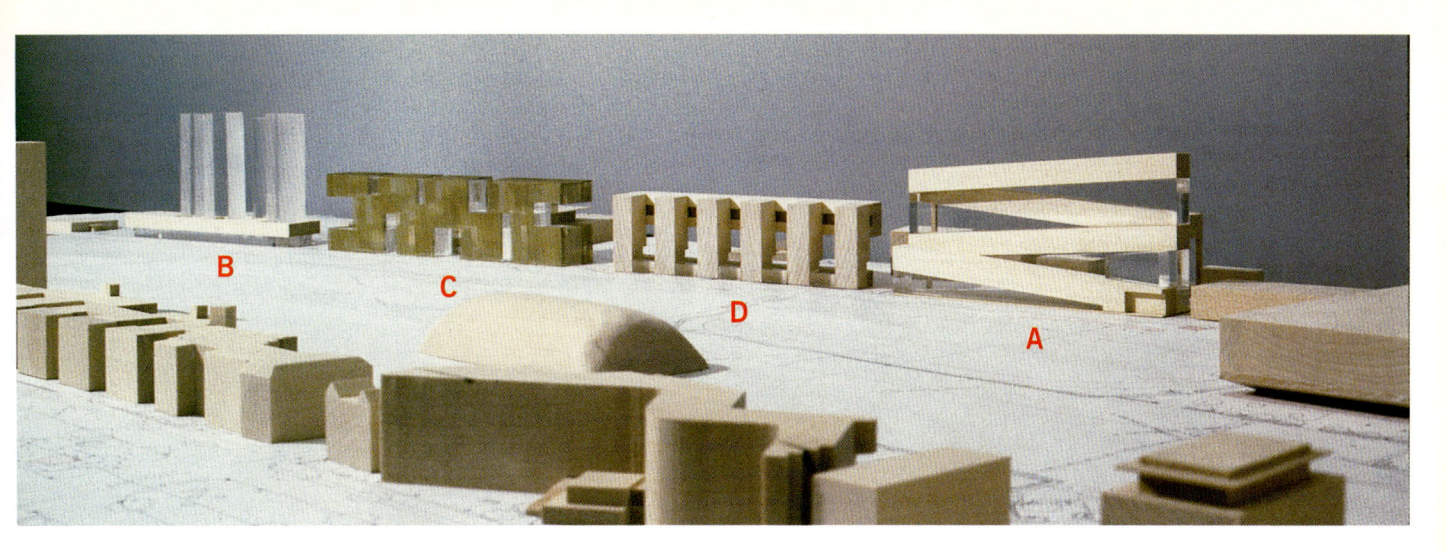

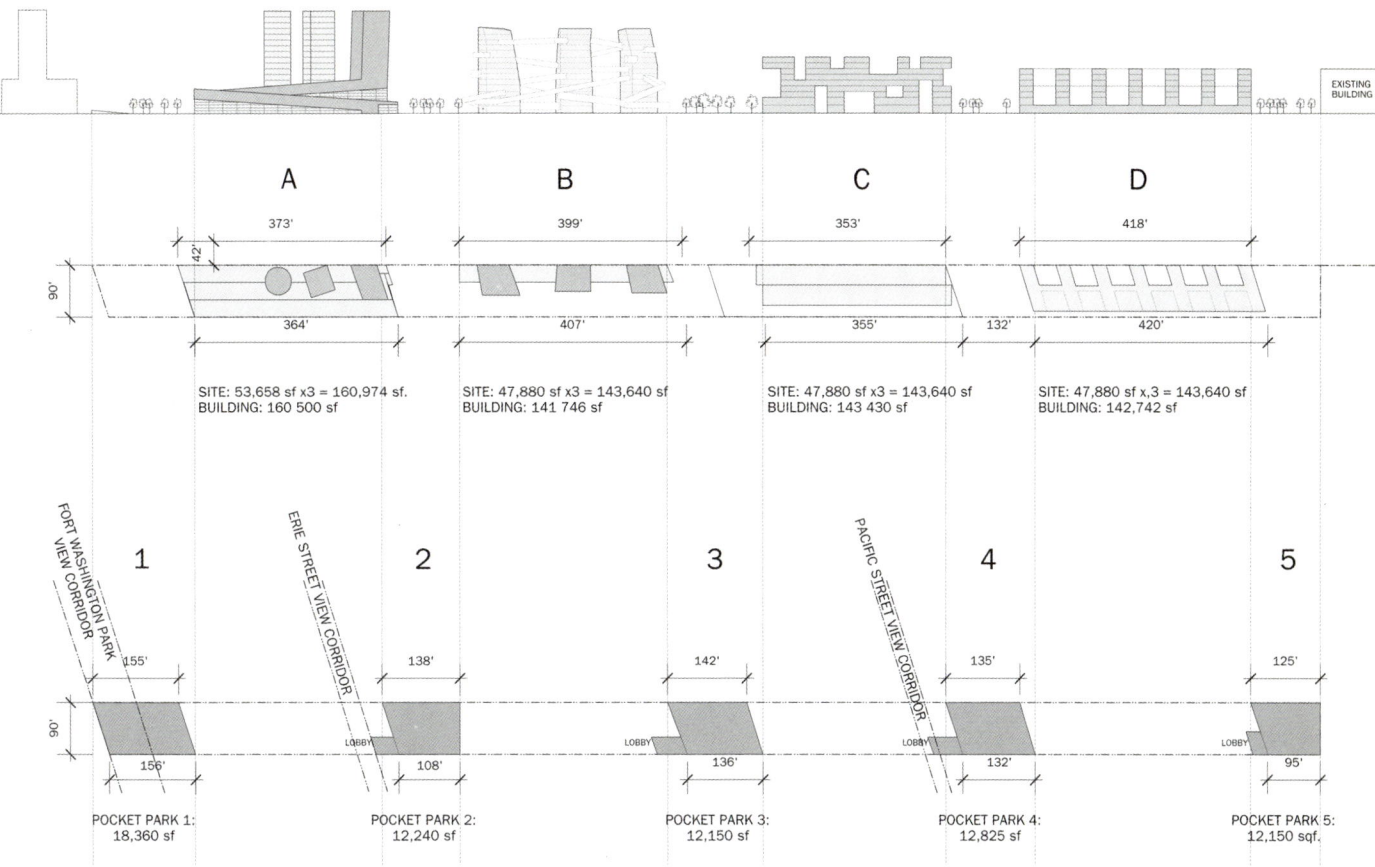

	A	B	C	D
Width (top)	373'	399'	353'	418'
Width (bottom)	364'	407'	355'	132' / 420'
	42' / 90'			
SITE	53,658 sf x3 = 160,974 sf.	47,880 sf x3 = 143,640 sf	47,880 sf x3 = 143,640 sf	47,880 sf x,3 = 143,640 sf
BUILDING	160 500 sf	141 746 sf	143 430 sf	142,742 sf

	1	2	3	4	5
Top	155'	138'	142'	135'	125'
Bottom	156'	108'	136'	132'	95'
	POCKET PARK 1: 18,360 sf	POCKET PARK 2: 12,240 sf	POCKET PARK 3: 12,150 sf	POCKET PARK 4: 12,825 sf	POCKET PARK 5: 12,150 sqf.

View corridors: FORT WASHINGTON PARK VIEW CORRIDOR, ERIE STREET VIEW CORRIDOR, PACIFIC STREET VIEW CORRIDOR

TOP: Master plan, study model
BOTTOM: Master plan, study showing proposed buildings and pocket parks

opposite:
Simmons Hall, Vassar Street corridor study

MASTER PLAN

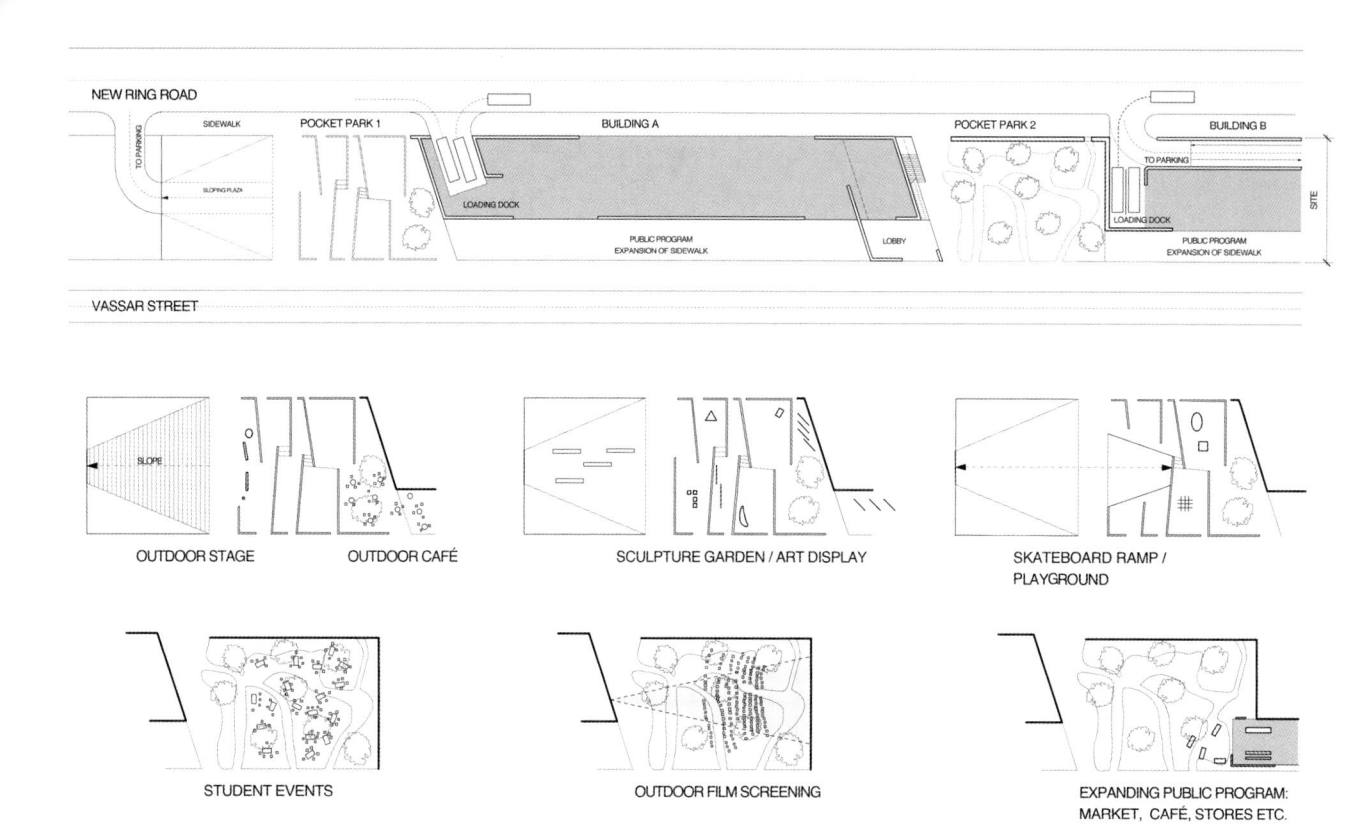

Individuation of pocket parks

32 MASTER PLAN

Pocket parks, watercolor study

INDIVIDUATION OF THE POCKET PARKS

Just as the buildings are conceived of as "Houses of Individuation," the parks should also be individuated. By relating the design of the park to the design of the building through concept, materials, and details, it increases the residents' sense of ownership of the landscape as well as enlivening the streetscape along Vassar Street. We envision each park to be directly connected to the building entry adjacent to it, thus fostering this relationship between the residents and the parks.

Pocket Parks can be individuated through:

CONCEPT OF RELATED BUILDING GEOMETRY
Shape of space
Warped ground plane
Water ponds or small fountains

PLANTINGS
Height and mass of plants
Shape and texture
Seasonal changes of color

OUTDOOR PROGRAMMING
Study seating benches
Movies projected onto adjacent buildings
Performance stage and bench seating
Barbeque pit

MASTER PLAN 33

FOLDED STREET

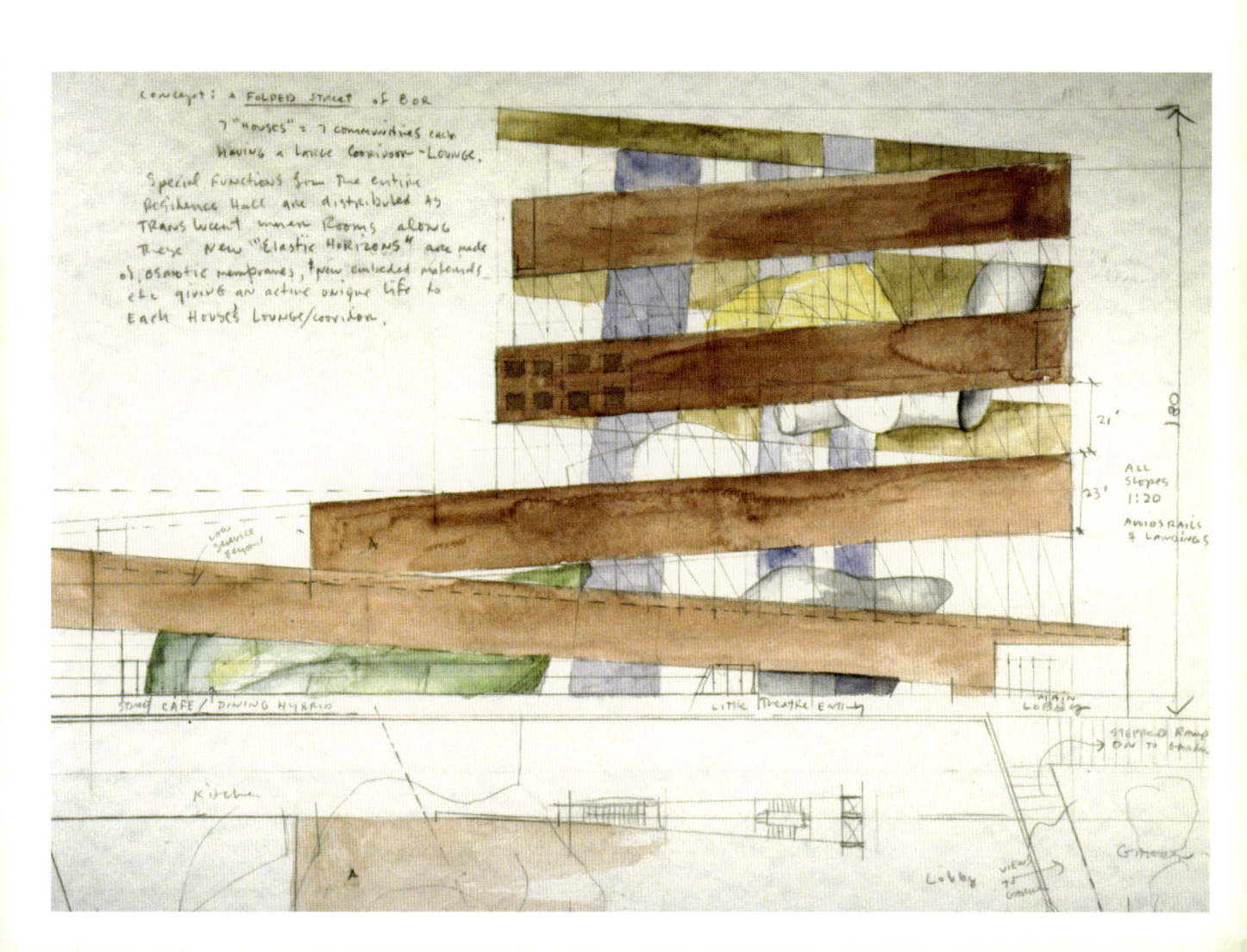

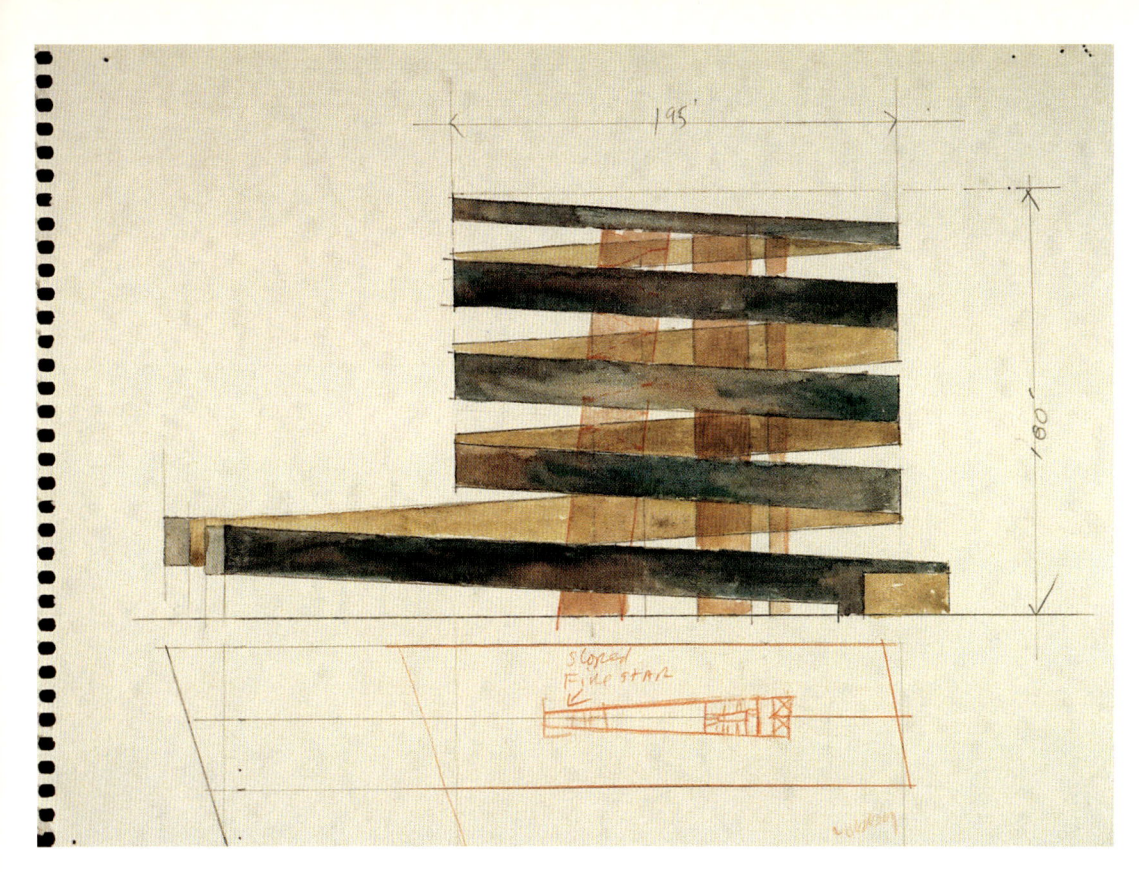

BUILDING CONCEPTS: FOLDED STREET

A folded street made of "houses," each a community with 35–40 students. The double-level house sections are interwoven with double-level glass lounge-corridors.

The program for a 350-bed undergraduate residence hall is nearly the same as the nearby Baker House (A. Aalto, 1949). Undergraduate students living in their first year away from home have an urgent need to socialize and make new friends, which is frustrated by 24-hour-a-day work schedules.

The folded street concept maximizes potential daily social interaction as it merges corridor-lounge activities in a loft of light-washed space. Views across Brigg's Field to the Charles River increase as the folds switch back to rise in eight "houses" reaching 180' in height. The lower floors offer south sun terraces that gradually slope down to a pocket park full of benches for outdoor study.

Along the glass lounge-corridors, a translucent membrane of inner rooms can accommodate the private activities of a little performance theater, laundry rooms, kitchens, etc.

opposite:
Folded street scheme, conceptual watercolor

ADVANTAGES OF THE SLOPE-SHEARED SECTION

1. CORRIDOR LOUNGE:

Access to the private space is through the public space. All movement activates the public space and creates the third quality of social condensing (meeting) space.

2. POROSITY:

Through the slope-sheared section sun shines through the full 60' building section creating a porous structure.

3. CONTINUOUS RESIDENCE HALL:

Public space is a continuous string of spaces that winds through the building, binding the seven separate houses into a whole residence.

4. *Through the slope there is an individuality of entrances. The personal rooms have variety here.*

5. *Public space is always opposite private space.*

6. *Space is continuously changing.*

Folded street scheme, conceptual watercolor

FOLDED STREET

SH: At the time, we felt that the folded street was the strongest of the four ideas. We were very interested with the notion of bringing the urban life of the street up into the building. Structurally, the rooms would hang from large trusses. The scheme maintains our desire for porosity by stretching apart the components of a more normative scheme, allowing a visual connection to the neighborhoods to the north and flooding the interior with natural light.

The project was very well developed. A model had been built, the program was worked out, and we had a structural concept for the trusses. Things were going very well and everyone was very excited about the scheme, but there was a problem. The as-of-right building code specified a one hundred-foot maximum height along Vassar Street. At the outset of the project, we were assured that MIT would secure a variance for our 180-foot scheme. However, after four months of design development work, we were given an ultimatum. MIT would not pursue the variance, so we would have to revise the scheme to fall within the height restriction. To try to compress the folded street scheme to less than 100 feet simply would not work, so we were left with a simple but difficult choice; we could start over, or we could resign.

It was June 30, 1999. Schematic Design would have to be complete by September 1, and we were exhausted. I came back to New York and gathered the office around this very table. I felt that the decision had to be made by the group—I had no right to decide for the entire team—so we took a vote. The vote was fourteen to one in favor of continuing. Mine was the sole dissenting opinion.

TG: **Was this because you felt that the folded street would have resulted in a stronger building?**

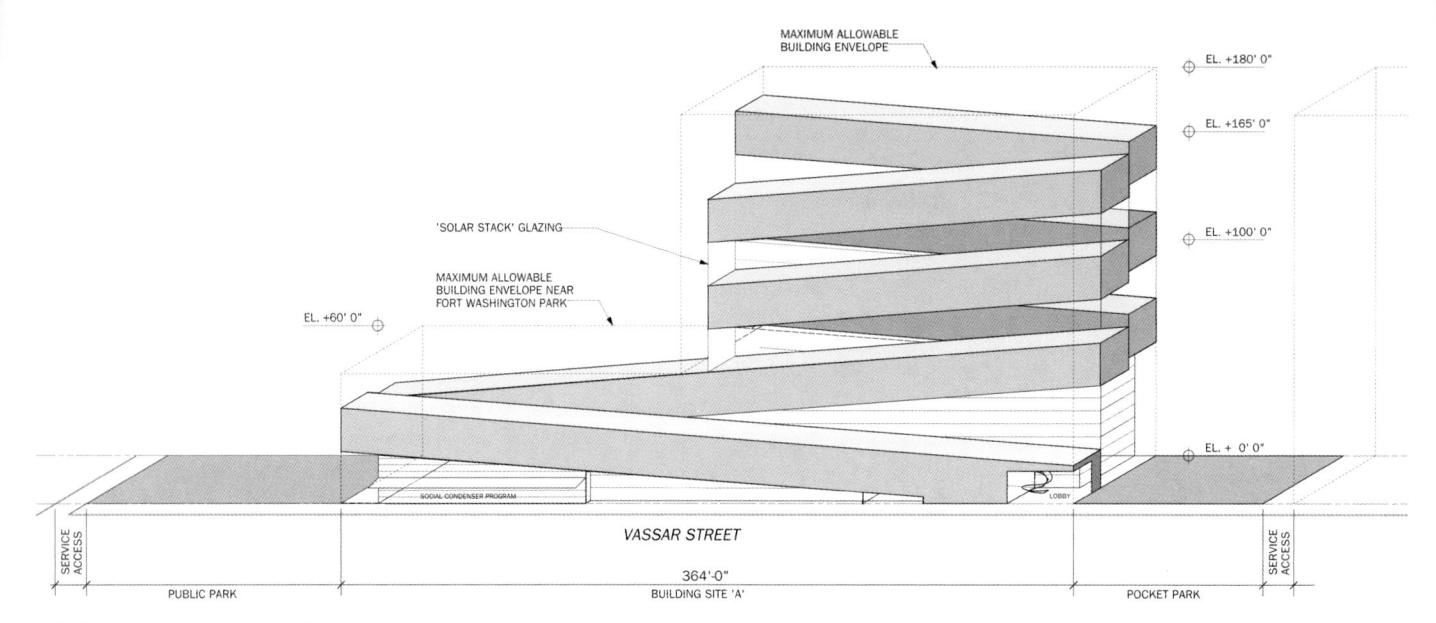

Folded street scheme, conceptual diagram

SH: I don't like to look back and wonder what might have been. I think what we built is much more than the folded street could have been. There are so many different scales at play—the urban scale, the scale of the individual, the scale of the detail. I voted no for selfish reasons, because I didn't want to give up my summer vacation. At the time, it was devastating to lose the folded street, but I believe we got a much stronger work of architecture in the end.

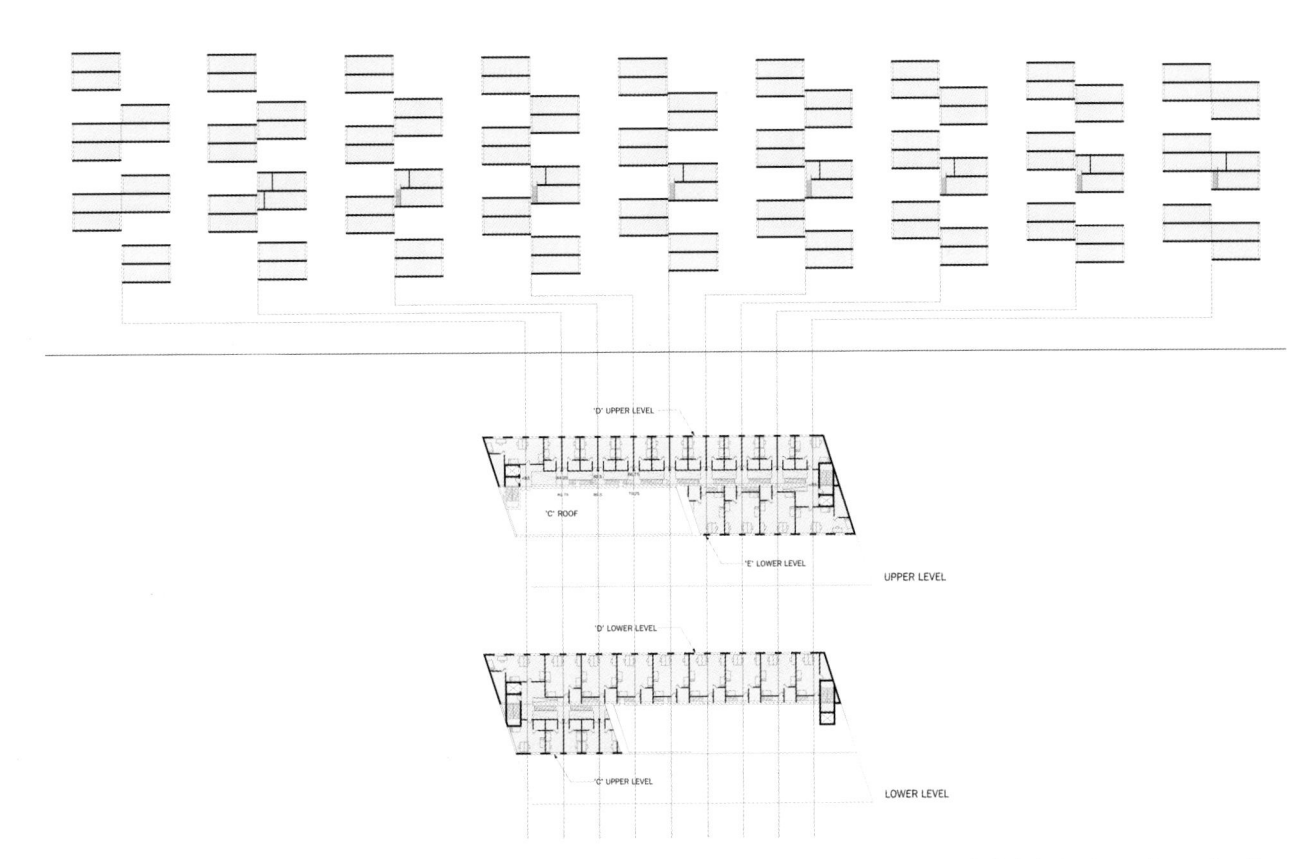

Folded street scheme, plans and sections

FOLDED STREET 41

HOUSE Ⓐ
LOUNGE CORRIDOR

PERFORATED
ACOUSTIC
PLYWOOD

TRANSLUCENT
GLASS WALL
SHOWS LIFE
OF ROOMS
BEYOND

VIEW TO
MIT DOME

"QUANTUM
FOAM"
FICTIONAL
EMBEDDED
SEATING

VIEW
CHARLES
RIVER

LOUNGE / EXERCISE ROOM

ABOVE LEFT: Folded street scheme, Schematic model, night view
ABOVE RIGHT: Folded street scheme, Schematic model, detail

opposite:
TOP and BOTTOM: Folded street scheme, conceptual watercolors of interior

Folded street scheme, schematic model,
overall view

opposite:
Folded street scheme, schematic model,
overall view

44 FOLDED STREET

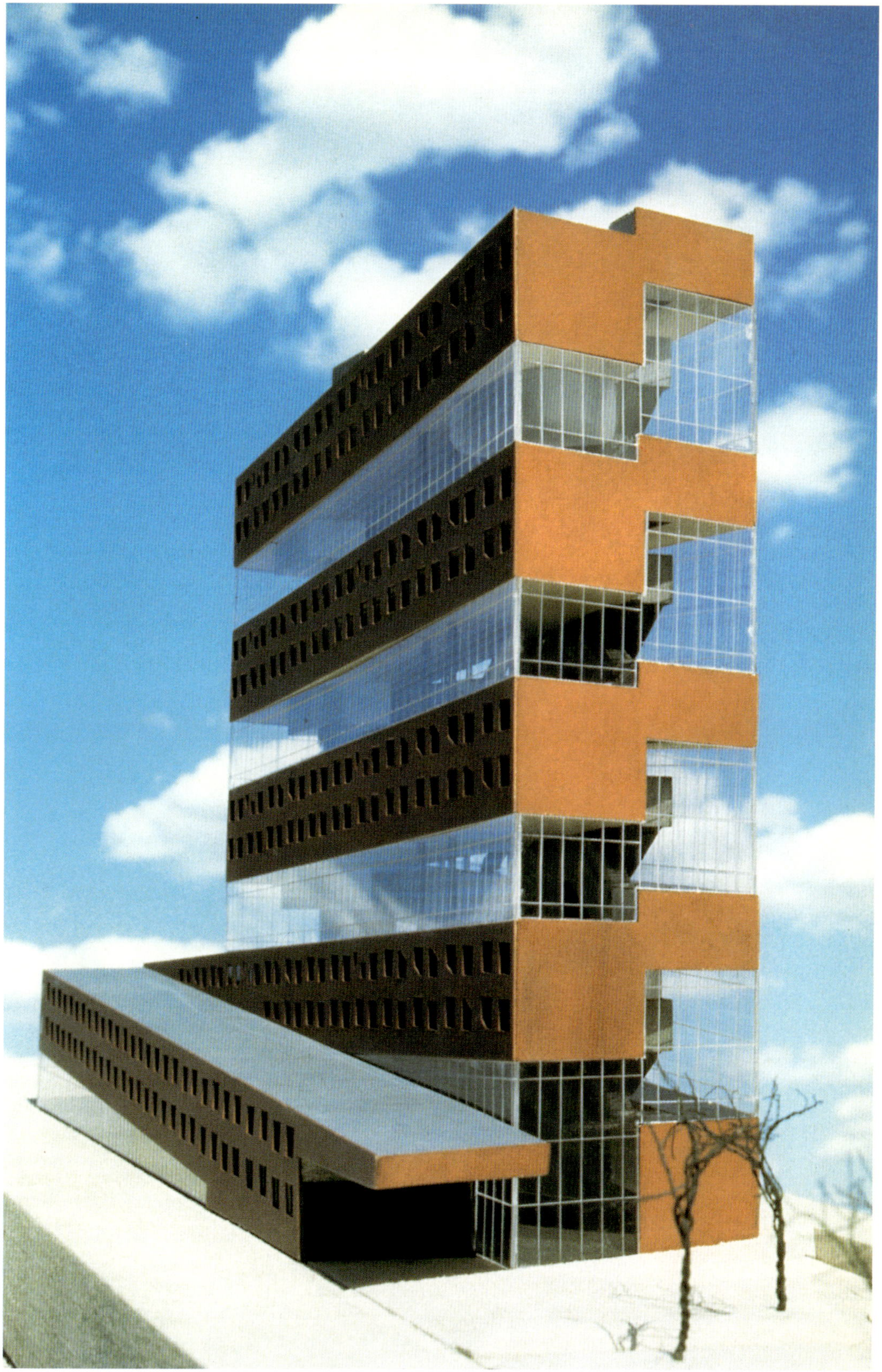

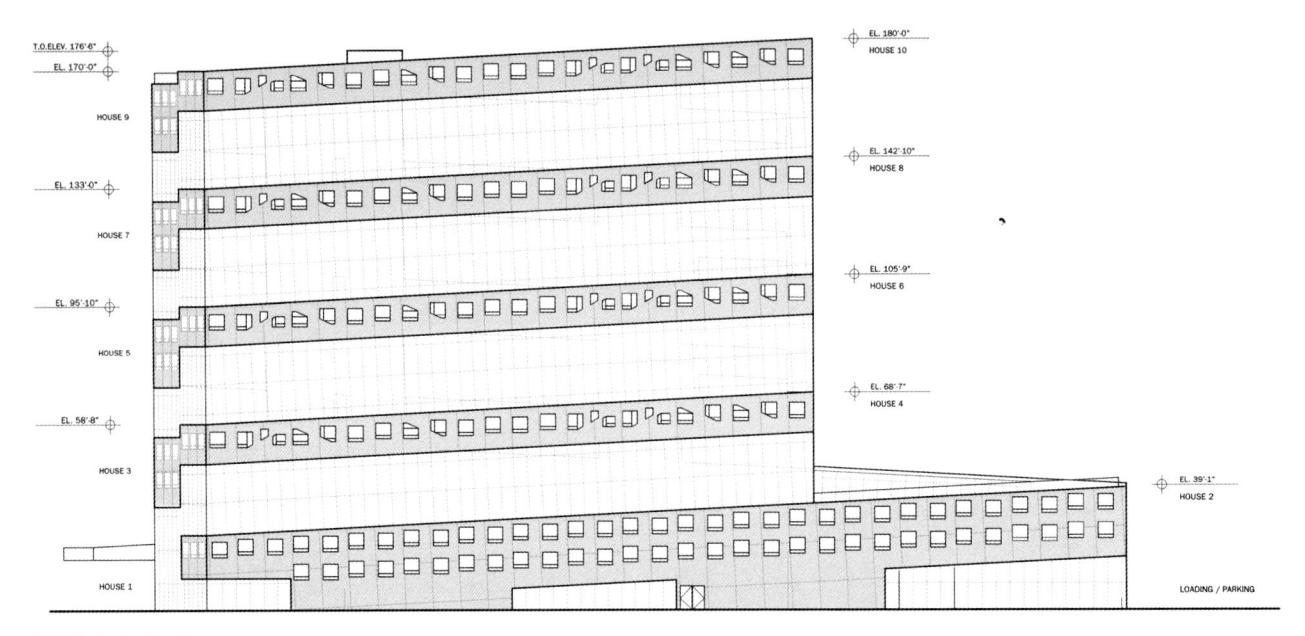

ABOVE: North elevation
BELOW: Typical floor plan

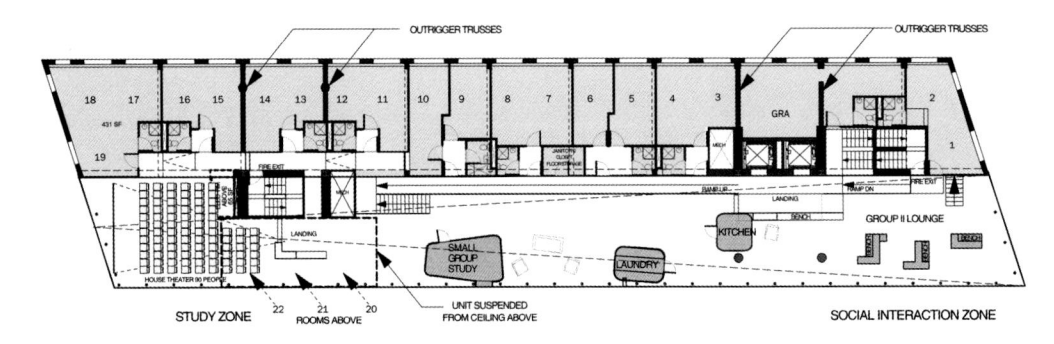

46 FOLDED STREET

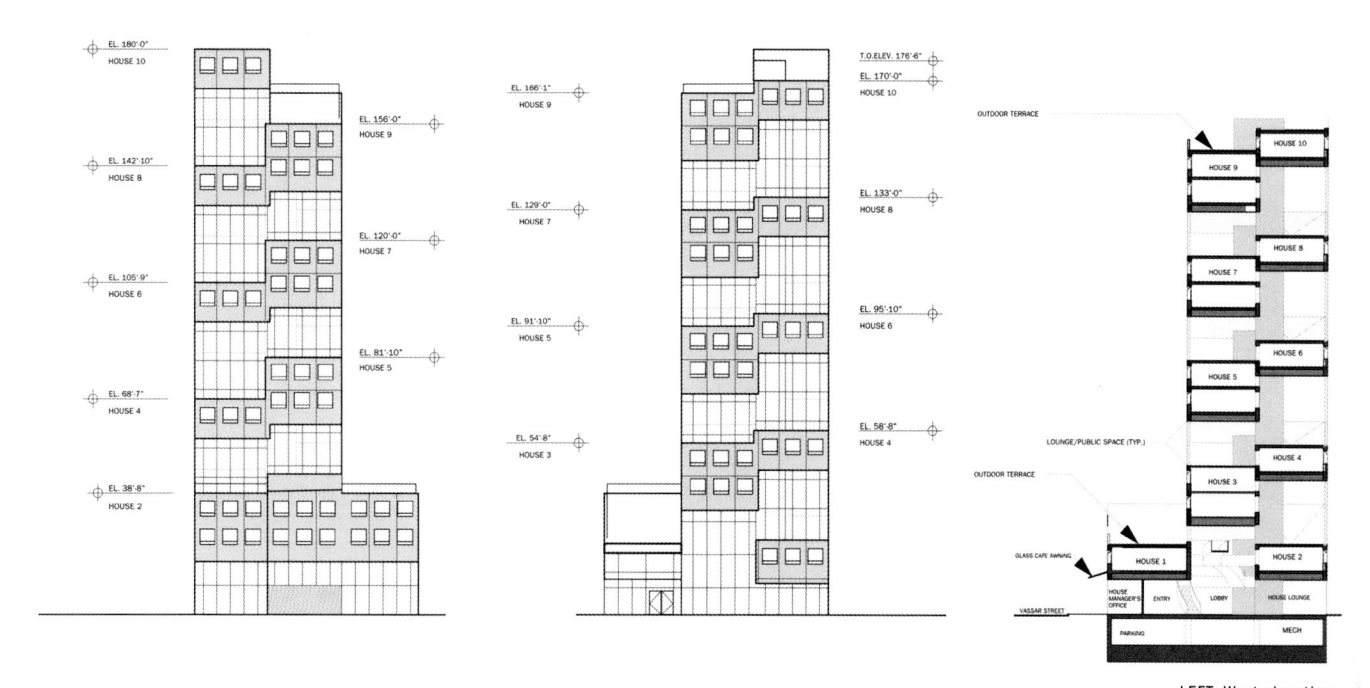

LEFT: West elevation
CENTER: East elevation
RIGHT: Section, facing east

FOLDED STREET 47

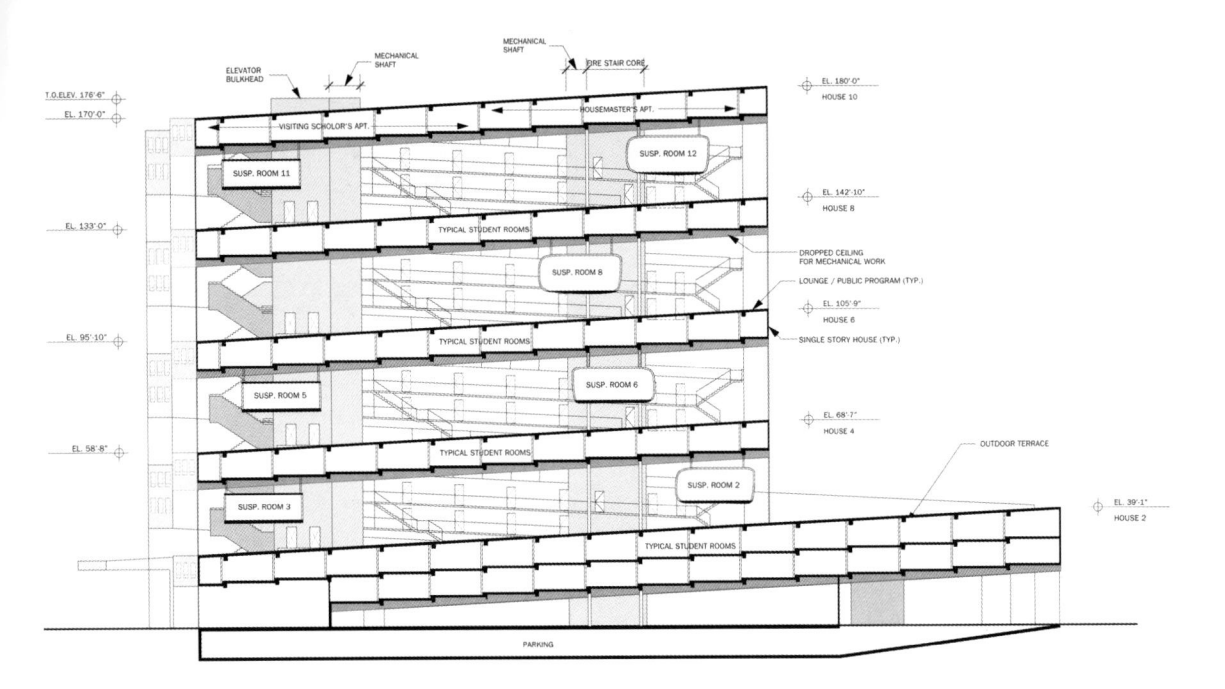

Section, facing south

48 FOLDED STREET

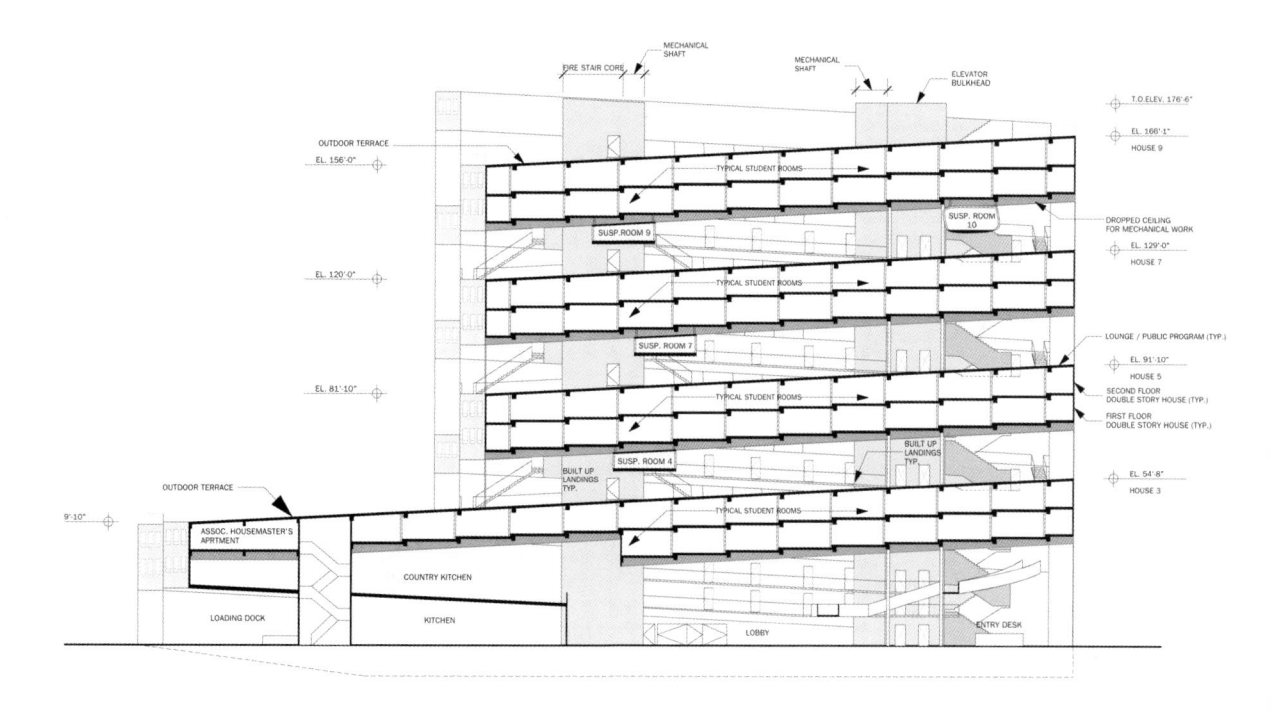

ABOVE: Section, facing north
BELOW: Section, through base

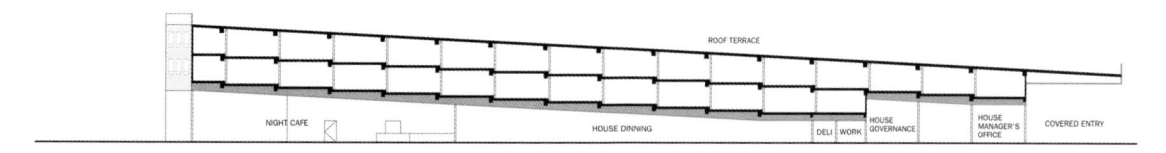

FOLDED STREET 49

SPONGE

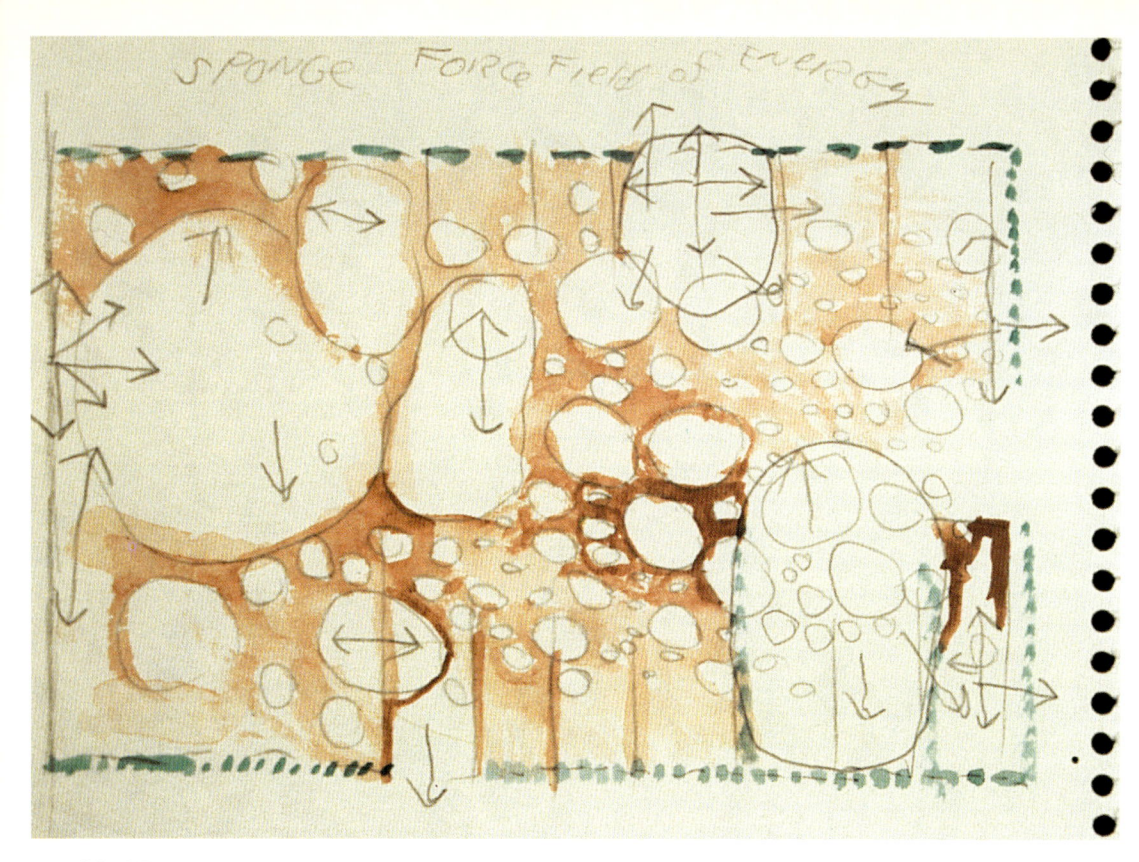

CONCEPT

The Sponge concept for the new undergraduate residence hall transforms a porous building morphology via a series of programmatic and biotechnical functions.

opposite:
Sponge space, watercolor concept sketch

SPONGE BUILDING

TG: This is an interesting drawing (opposite) to me because there is no indication of the corridor. It implies that circulation always occurs by moving through these sponge spaces.

SH: This sketch came very early on. You are right, I was trying to think about the building in a new way; I certainly did not start with the idea of a double-loaded corridor in my brain. I wanted something much more open-ended and unprecedented.

TG: I find that interesting. Given your early interest in problems of typology, it is tempting to think of the building as a critique of the double-loaded corridor building type. But in fact you are working in the opposite direction.

SH: True, I have a previous history in which much of my work was concerned with typology and morphology. Two issues of Pamphlet Architecture, *The Alphabetical City* (1980) and *Rural and Urban House Types* (1983), were primarily concerned with these issues. But in 1984 I discovered the work of Maurice Merleau-Ponty, and I radically altered my methods for making and understanding architecture.

TG: How so?

SH: My early work always began with typology. But after working through the writings of Merleau-Ponty, I began to develop a position in which a project could derive from concepts outside of architecture. You can see a distinct shift in the trajectory of my work around 1984 and '85. I began to play with the possibility that any conceptual strategy, if properly harnessed, could be used as a point of departure for architecture.

TG: Which project would you say best illustrates this shift?

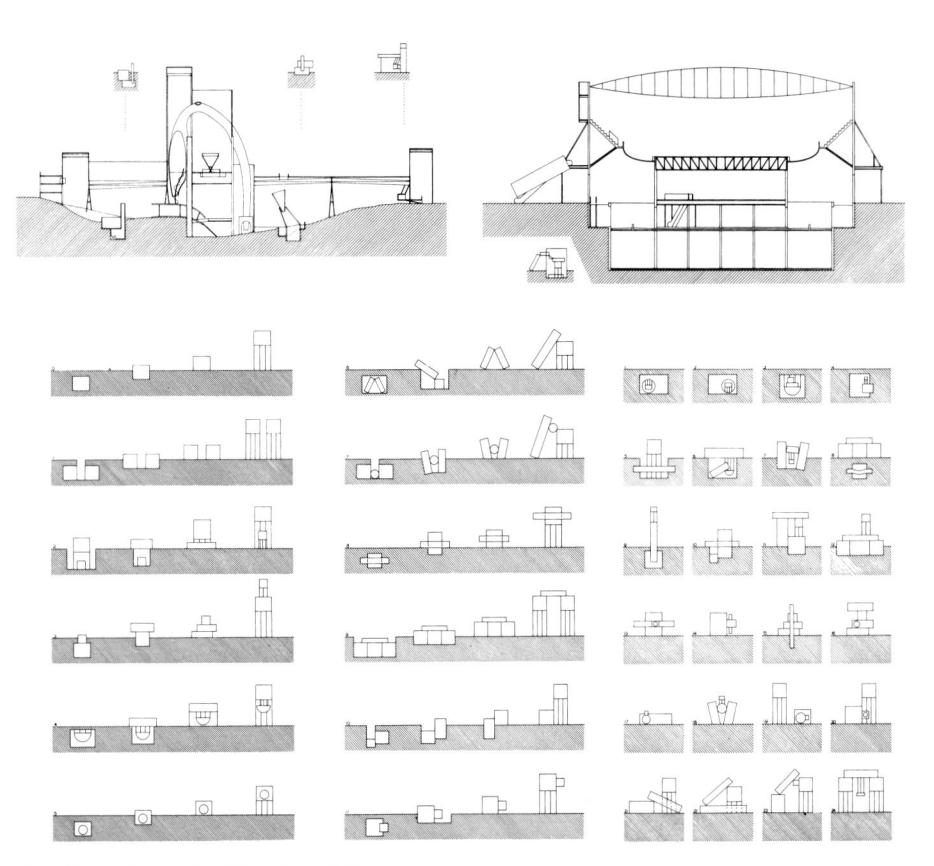

Porta Vittoria Competition, Milan, Italy, 1986,
diagrams of spatial relationships

54 SPONGE

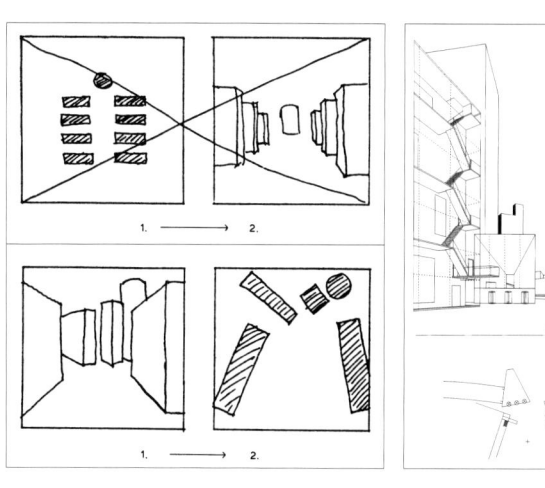

LEFT: Porta Vittoria Competition, diagrams from perspective to space
RIGHT: Porta Vittoria Competition, plan generated from perspective drawing

SH: The 1986 competition for the Porta Vittoria district in Milan. We were up against these Italian Rationalists, like Emilio Battisti, who would certainly be starting with a typological investigation. So we decided that we should begin from a different place. We didn't know exactly what we would do, but we knew it would not begin with typology.

I believe that what an artist refuses to do is just as important as what an artist does, perhaps more important. Much of my teaching involves urging students to avoid this or that cliché, to work instead from an original position. I cannot help but hear that same voice when I sit down at my own drawing board. For us, this decision to "avoid" became the driving force for constructing a new palette for making architecture.

A simple series of drawings from Porta Vittoria illustrates this new way of working. Rather than beginning with an established formal arrangement and then developing a familiar kind of space, we made perspective drawings first. From these, we worked in reverse, deriving plan arrangements from these initial sketches. This proved to be a useful technique that we still employ today; it keeps you from relying too heavily on the abstraction of the plan.

Even before the concrete idea has taken shape, we can sketch ideas for the spaces within a project. It is an intuitive process that begins before you have the whole. Stravinsky composed several important pieces of music in this way. The "beginning" of a project is very difficult to fix in time. It does not necessarily begin with the form or the idea or the sketch; it results from each of these coalescing in time.

We were fortunate to have six months to work on Porta Vittoria. Simmons Hall was under much more pressure, but, as evidenced by this early conceptual sketch, you can see a similar sort of investigation at work. Certainly typology finds its way in—it is inevitable—but we no longer allow typological thinking to be the driving force in our designs.

LEFT: Sea sponge
RIGHT: Sponge print on building footprint used to create public spaces

JK: **The first instance does not matter. The issue is one of forming a dialogue. I do not mean to diminish the pursuit of originality in one's work, I just think that originality does not thrive until a community of similar explorations develops.**

SH: Perhaps that is the case. Looking back, maybe we were racing with Morphosis and Mangurian to see who could produce the most obsessive models.

JK: **In the case of Simmons Hall, I see a relationship between your removal of building mass through the voids and the earth art of the 1970s. That was a period in art and architecture when many people were interested in excavation. Your project owes something to the advances made by such artists as James Turrell, Robert Smithson, and Gordon Matta-Clark, artists who challenged the notion of the earth as a neutral background for the construction of art. Their work makes ambiguous the naturalness of the earth as well as the artificiality of interventions upon it. It also provides an unconscious background to your work at MIT. It is not crucial, but it is important to recognize. Rather than characterize your project as something totally new, I prefer to think of it as a new way of working through an established problem.**

SH: Perhaps you are right, but constructing these histories is the job of critics. While we were certainly aware of these artists you mentioned, we were not overtly trying to participate in that discussion.

In fact, the conceptual beginnings of this project were quite humorous. At the beginning, I went out and bought a bunch of sea sponges. Sea sponges have a very complex, organic structure that exhibits an incredible variety of spaces. They are very different from synthetic kitchen and bath sponges.

I laid out the rectangle of the building footprint on my drawing table and made a series of ink drawings with the sponges—just smashing the sponge

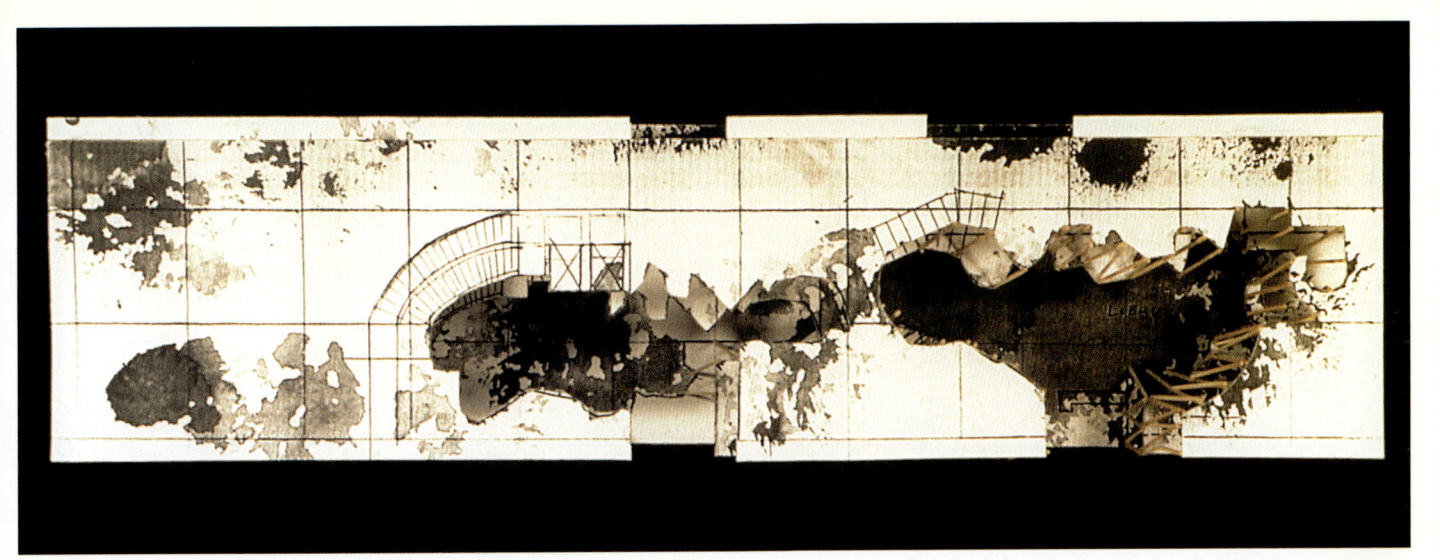

TOP and BOTTOM: Schematic model connecting sponge prints floor to floor

SPONGE 59

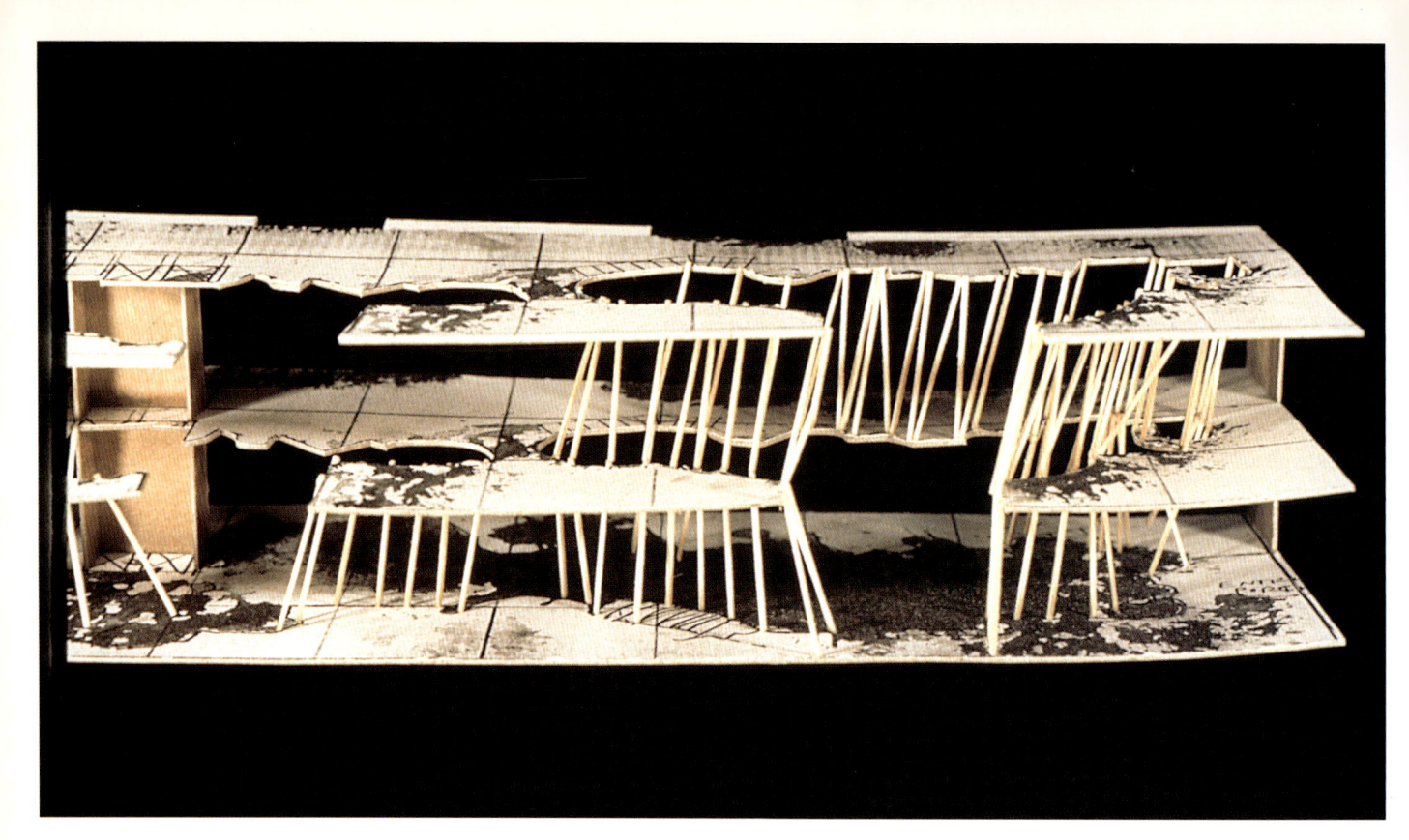

onto the page. Then I had to go to Europe. While I was gone, people in the office took those drawings and connected the different floor plans with ruled surfaces. Ours was a simple strategy: A typical C-stud will span twenty feet, easily through two floors of the building. So if we would blot these sponge imprints on every other floor, the mechanical process of connecting them with straight lines would generate the three-dimensional form. While I was away, the office generated a series of models that concretized the initial concept drawings.

The other benefit of the ruled surface was that it gave us a way to construct the building. In this manner, we could generate complex, doubly warped surfaces entirely out of straight lines. We did not have a large budget, and we wanted these complex forms, so devising a way to make them with everyday construction techniques and materials was the only option.

TG: **How do you know when you've got the shapes right?**

SH: You don't have them right for a very long time. There is a hell of a lot of program to push around within the building. First, we make these inspirational models and drawings, but the real toughness comes with the realities of the program. There was a very tight net-to-gross ratio we had to meet, so we only had so much area to play with.

I was looking for a way to make the public spaces of the building undeniable, even though they are quite small in terms of total building area. Drilling vertically through the floor slabs and defining these spaces with complex, doubly warped surfaces was a way to accomplish this. These amorphous voids became the lounge spaces, areas that were called for in the program. We could not afford to add space to the project, so the voids had to be necessary program elements. There were ten houses within the dorm, so we made ten lounges.

Sectional view of schematic model with sponge spaces

opposite:
Schematic model connecting sponge prints floor to floor

But the shapes are not right until the project is fully developed. Actually, they continue to be adjusted even into the construction process. Design development, by the way, is one of the most difficult and sensitive parts of architecture. Just look at the work of James Stirling. The early drawings in a project are often quite ugly, but through the development process, he gets it. So you don't have to be worried about getting it right, you just have to have the confidence—perhaps call it arrogance—that the idea can propel the project to completion. Along the way, you have to be willing to constantly tinker with the forms, to push and pull them as the program and structure dictate. And of course, through this process you will make discoveries that will inspire you to pursue other possibilities.

TG: In early drawings, you note that the void spaces would act as the lungs of the building (see p. 57), drawing air up through the building with fans and releasing it through the roof. Also, photovoltaic cells

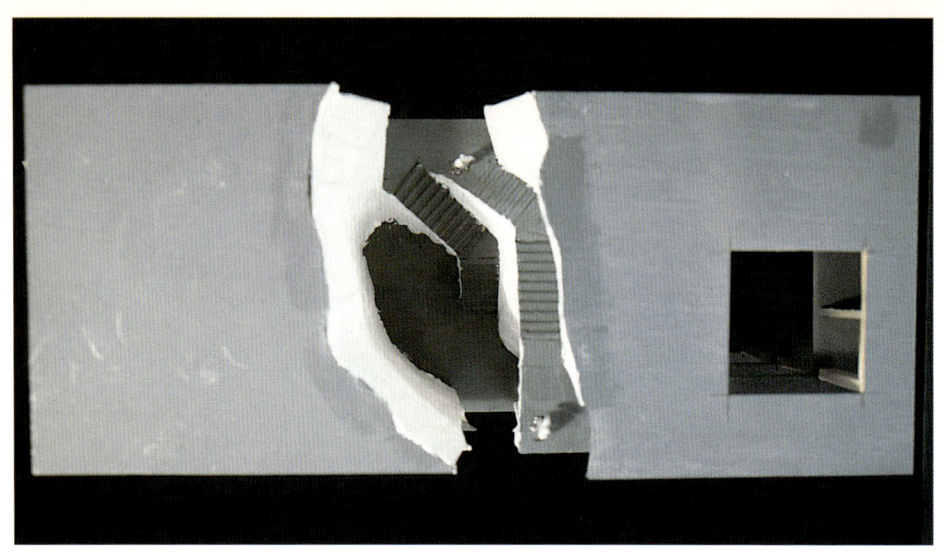

LEFT and RIGHT: Study models

were to provide power to these fans and other building systems. Are these the sorts of possibilities you are talking about?

SH: Yes. But alas, not all of these ideas made it into the realized building. The upper void spaces do open up through the roof, but fire codes would not allow us to connect the voids through all the floors; we were forced to provide smoke partitions between them. The photovoltaic cells represented a $250,000 deduction for MIT. Of course, they can be added back later, but with Boston's sunlight through the school year, it probably will not happen. The challenge is not only to find these possibilities; you have to make sure that they are a rational decision for the institution to make.

Beyond functional possibilities, design possibilities also become apparent. As we worked, a member of the team asked if it was okay for the void shapes to intersect the student rooms. "Sure," I said, "the students will love it." In fact, if you visit the building, you will find students who are very proud of their rooms. They want to show these strange shapes to visitors. Those are the happiest kids in the dormitory.

Strangely, the committee at MIT was initially opposed to these intersections. But the time constraints of the project worked to our advantage. If there were more time, we would have had to go through many more design reviews with the client, and these kinds of committees tend to dilute ideas in a work of architecture. On a tight schedule, you can avoid all these compromises.

TOP LEFT: Section model, detail
TOP RIGHT: Section model, detail showing sponge spaces
BOTTOM: Conceptual watercolor of corridor interrupted by organic public space

SPONGE 63

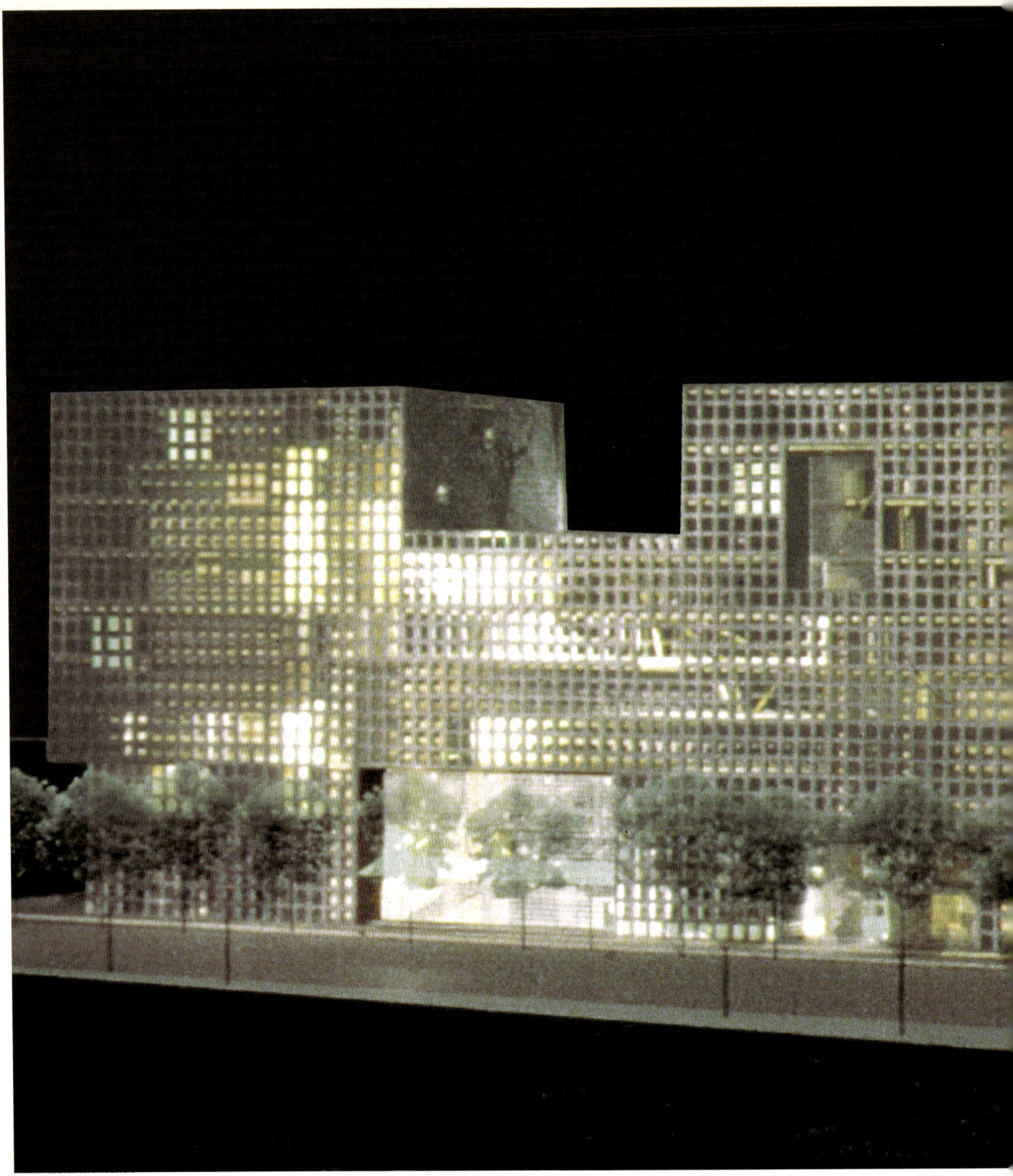

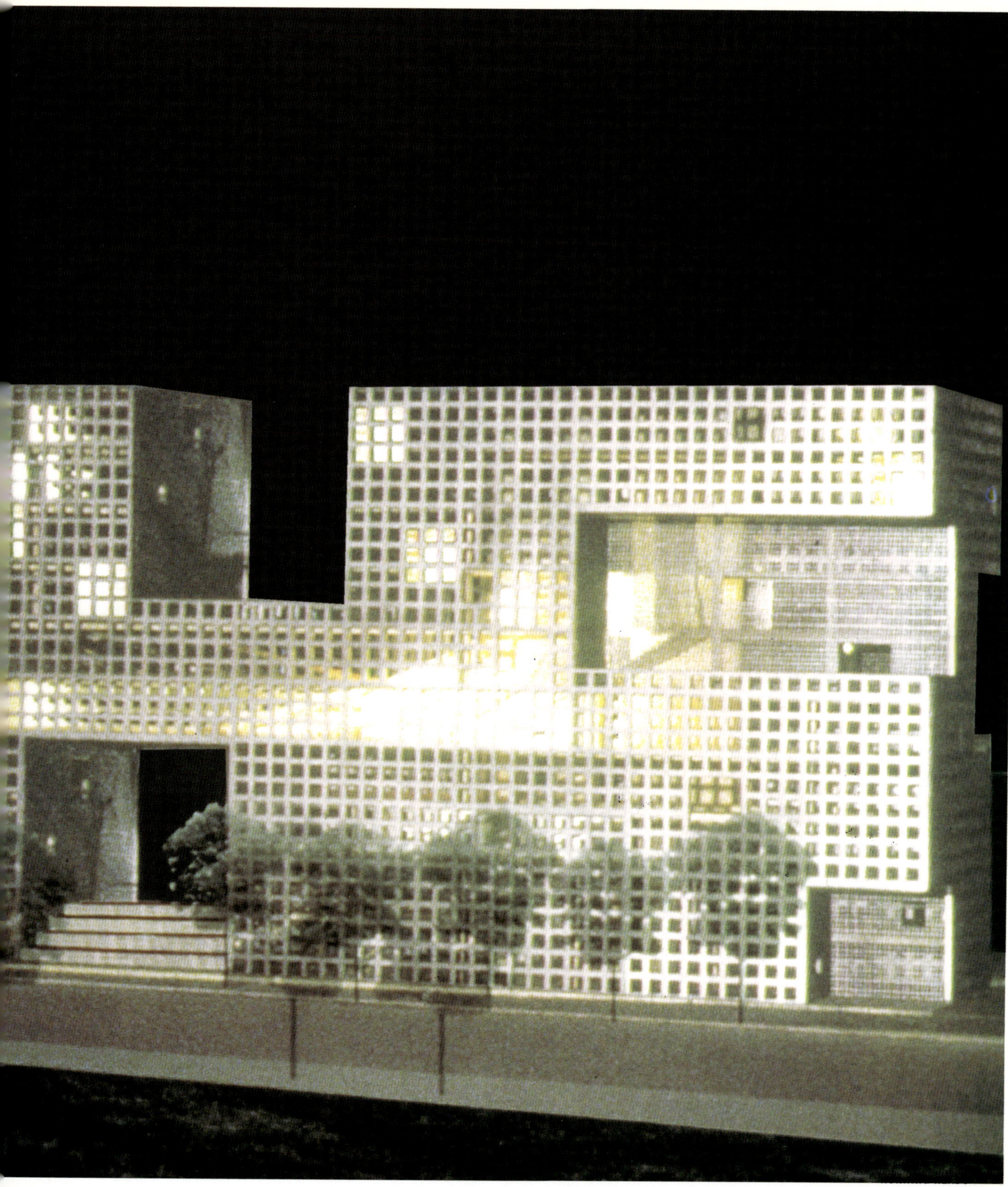

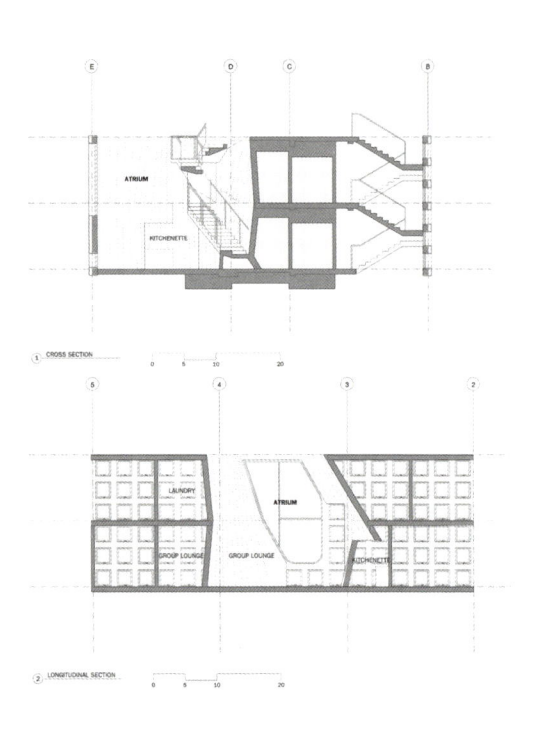

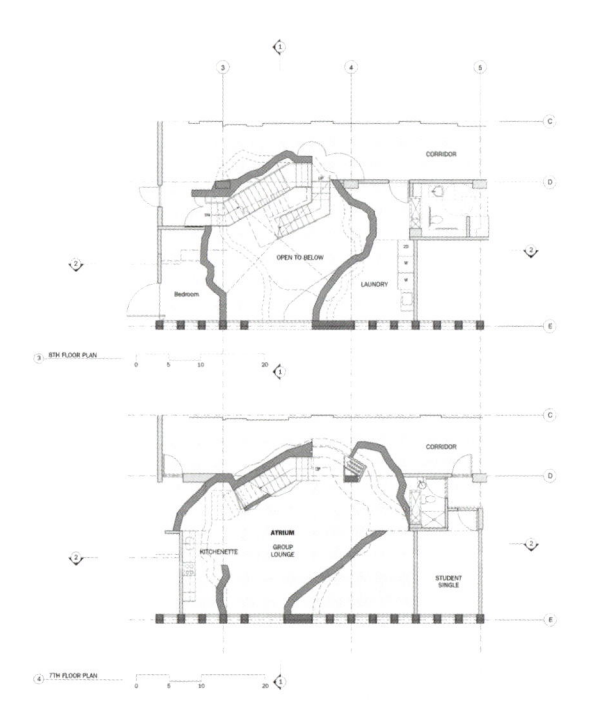

TOP: Schematic model
BOTTOM: Plans and sections

66 SPONGE

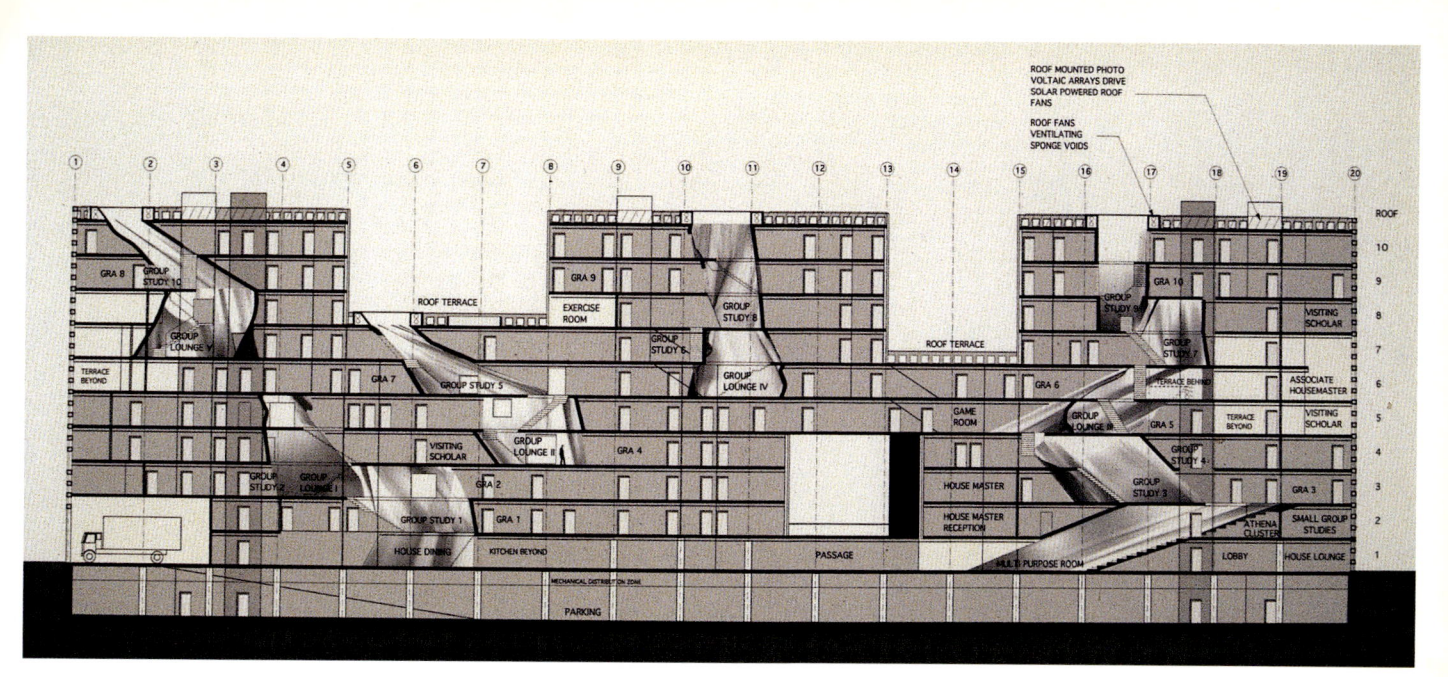

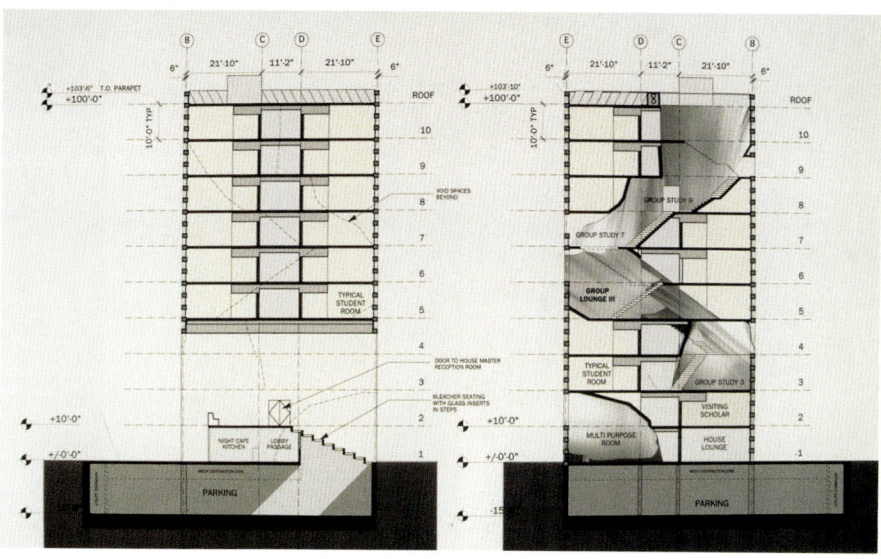

TOP: Schematic longitudinal section
BOTTOM: Schematic cross sections

SPONGE 67

Simmons Hall, view of main entrance

opposite:
Simmons Hall, conceptual watercolor, exterior view

The 350-bed residence is envisioned as part of the city form and campus form with a concept of "porosity" along Vassar Street. It is a vertical slice of a city ten stories tall and 382' long. The Urban Concept provides amenities such as a 125-seat theater, as well as a night cafe. House dining is on street level, like a street-front restaurant with a special awning and outdoor tables. The corridors connecting the rooms are like streets (8 feet wide) which happen upon urban experiences. As in Aalto's Baker House, the hallway can be more like a public place, a lounge.

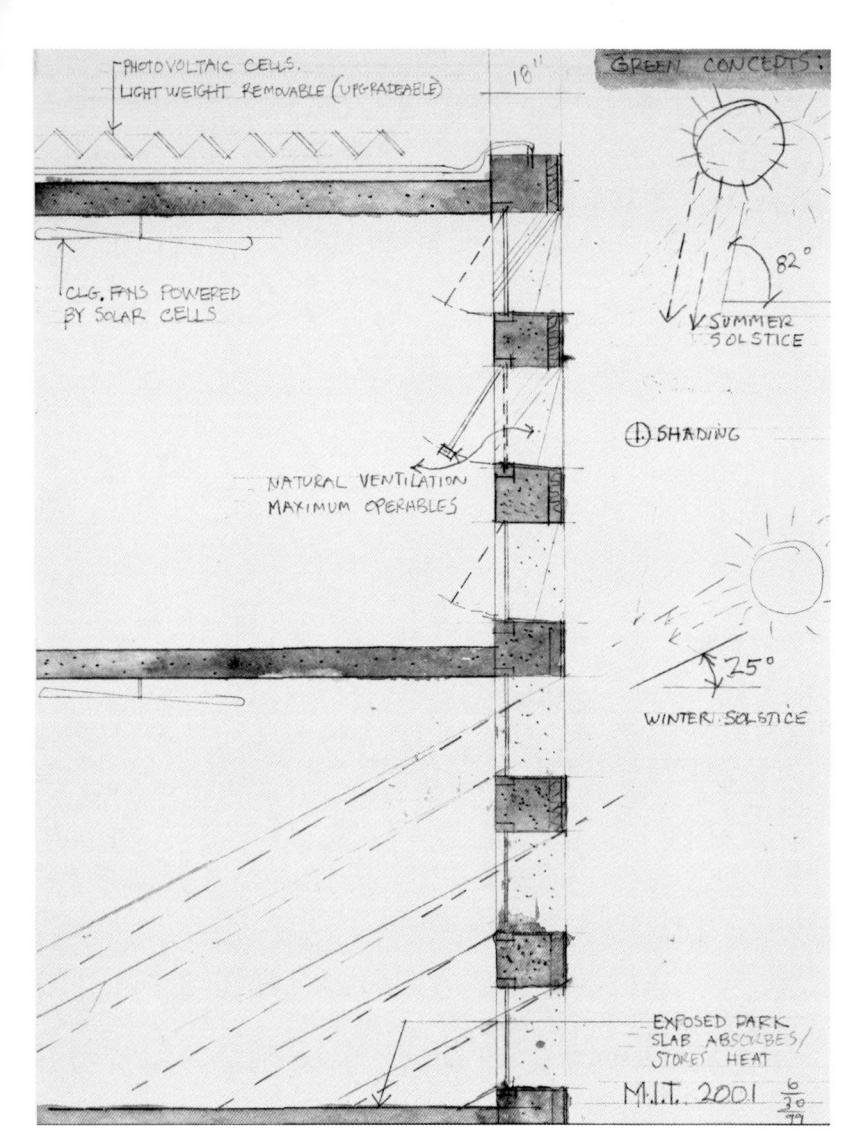

The "perfcon" structure is a unique design, allowing for maximum flexibility and interaction. Each of the dormitory's single rooms has nine operable windows over 2' x 2' in size. The 12' depth of the wall naturally shades out the summer sun, while allowing the low-angled winter sun in to help heat the building.

ABOVE: Perfcon, section study

opposite:
Window detail

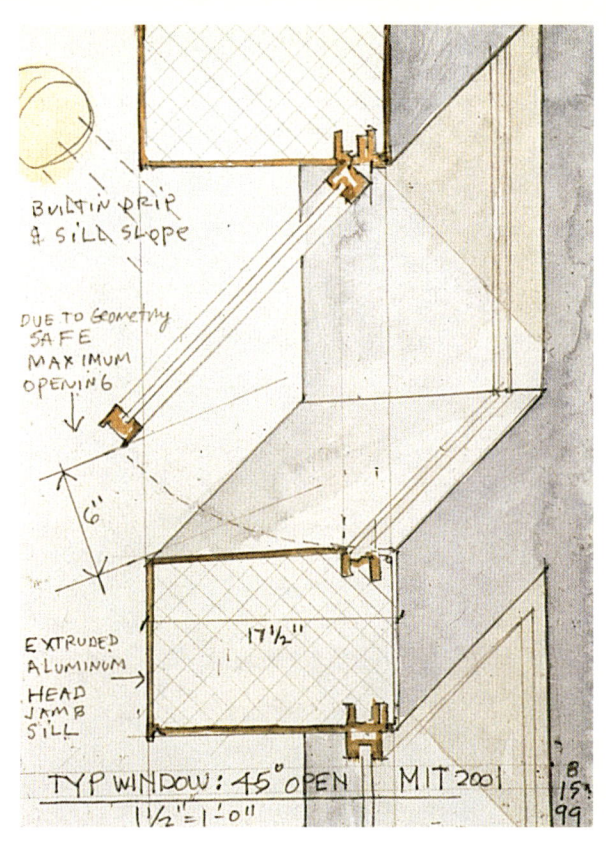

PERFCON

TG: Along with the concrete void spaces, another important component of the building is the concrete building envelope. At what point does the materiality of the building enter into the design process?

SH: Very early on. The planning department originally wanted to do the building in steel, as did Perry Dean Rogers, our associate architect in Boston. We were, as I said, under tight time constraints, and steel buildings tend to go up more quickly than concrete buildings. Nonetheless, Guy Nordenson, the structural engineer, and I were determined to make the building out of concrete.

TG: Why?

SH: It was a way to give the building a sense of mass. In terms of energy efficiency, it makes sense to have the mass of the building at the perimeter, to act as a natural insulator. Also, with the windows of the dorm rooms set back some twenty inches from the face of the wall, the thickness of the concrete would act as a sun shade, allowing the winter sun to enter but blocking the higher rays of the summer sun.

Conceptually, too, concrete made more sense. Had the building been constructed of steel, the depth of the facade would have to be built up with metal studs. But with the concrete system we used, the structure itself was a porous mass.

We devised a new method of precast concrete construction—Perfcon. The panels were all cast in Canada and shipped to the site. Each panel—there were six thousand of them—was unique, but they all came from the same form at the precaster's facility. Reinforcing steel was digitally coordinated and the process ran very smoothly. Coordinating the process digitally afforded an incredible precision to the project, a kind of digital supercharging. In terms

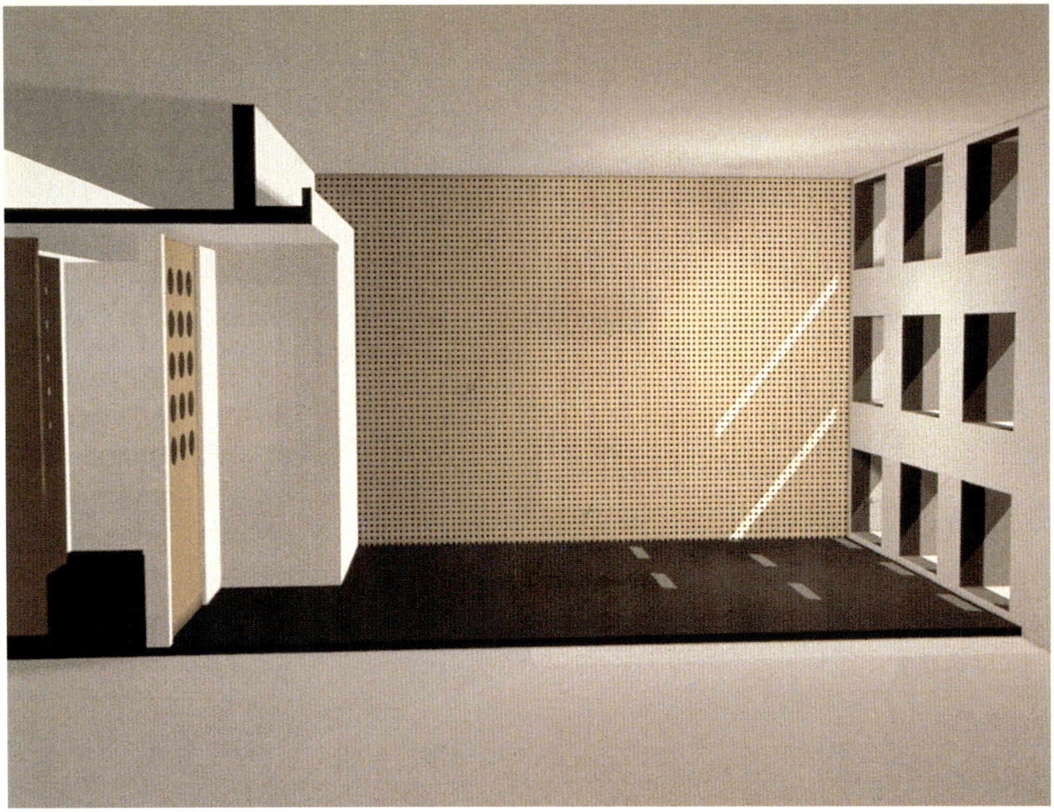
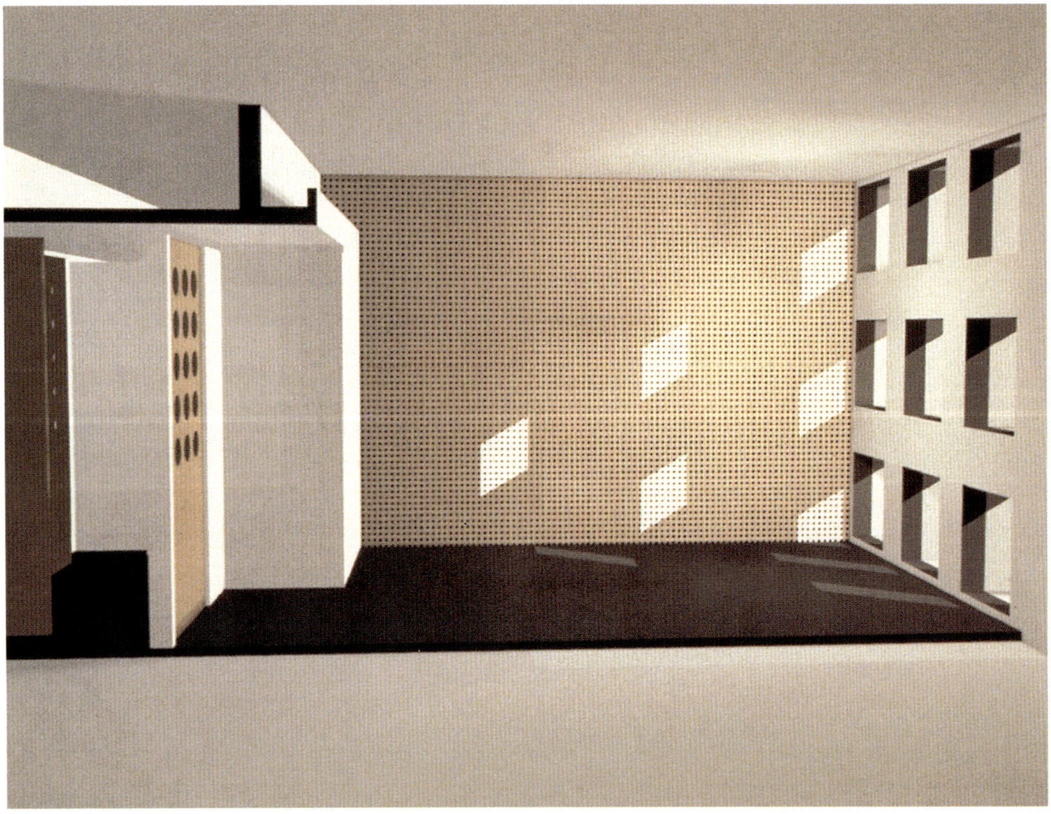

opposite:
TOP: Student room lighting study, vernal equinox
BOTTOM: Student room lighting study, winter solstice

of material and detail, this is the most experimental thing we did on the building.

TG: **Was it expensive?**

SH: No, these concrete panels were very economical. Through the design process, we had to run a concrete- and a steel-frame system side-by-side, and the most inexpensive system would be employed. We were very fortunate to find the Canadian precaster who did the work within the budget.

We were able to achieve an incredible precision because of the controlled conditions of the precaster and the accuracy of the computer. That digital supercharging allows one to achieve incredible craft. The concrete that came to this project from Canada is perfect. Only one of the six thousand panels was defective—it had a small chip. The site-case concrete, on the other hand, was very crude. We intentionally played up the difference between the two systems by lining the forms of the site-cast work with random boards.

TG: **The concrete of the Perfcon panels is only seen on the inside of the building. Would you have preferred to express the concrete on the exterior?**

SH: Revealing the concrete on the exterior was never an option because we had to insulate the building. I would love to make a building out of Perfcon in another climate, Florida perhaps, where the concrete could be exposed. Without the aluminum skin, this would be a very economical system, but we knew that would not be possible in Boston.

TG: **So the aluminum skin was a part of the project from the beginning.**

SH: Yes. I knew that at this quantity and budget, to have operable windows they would have to be aluminum. So the sanded-aluminum skin matches the materiality of the windows, affording the building a monolithic quality.

ABOVE and OPPOSITE: Structural diagrams showing individual Perfcon panels

74 PERFCON

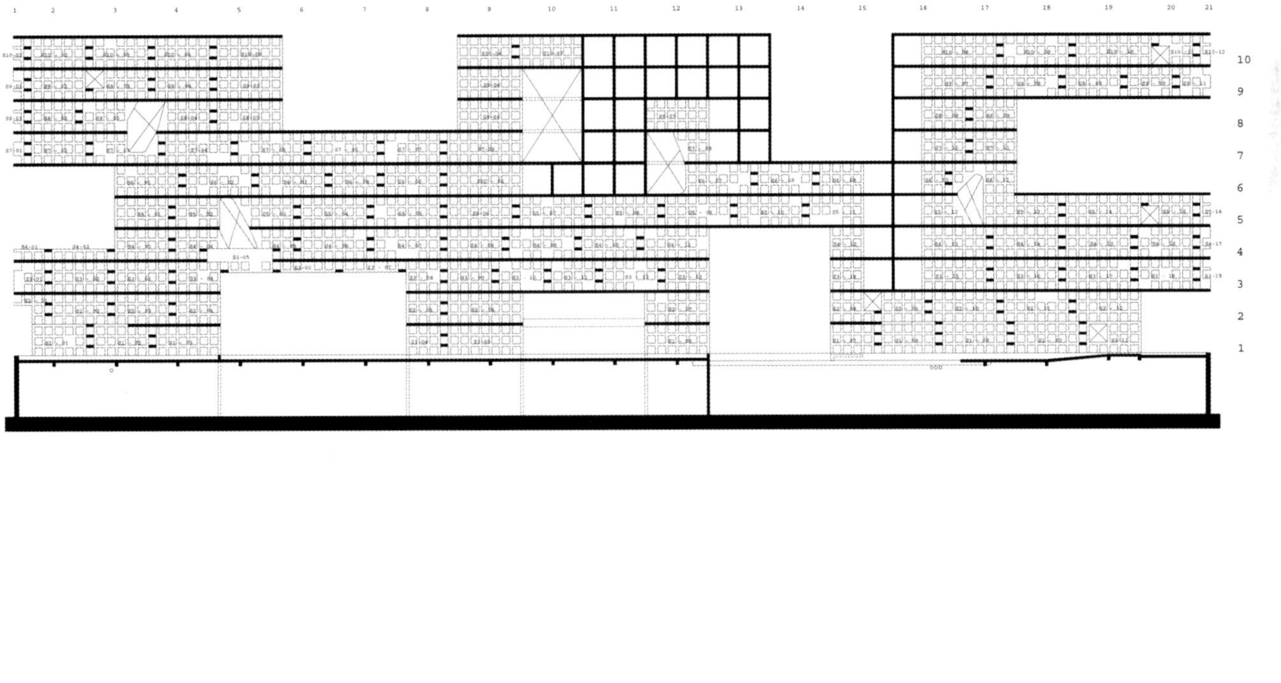
1
2
3
4
5
6
7
8
9
10
11
12
13
14
15
16
17
18
19
20
21
10
9
8
7
6
5
4
3
2
1

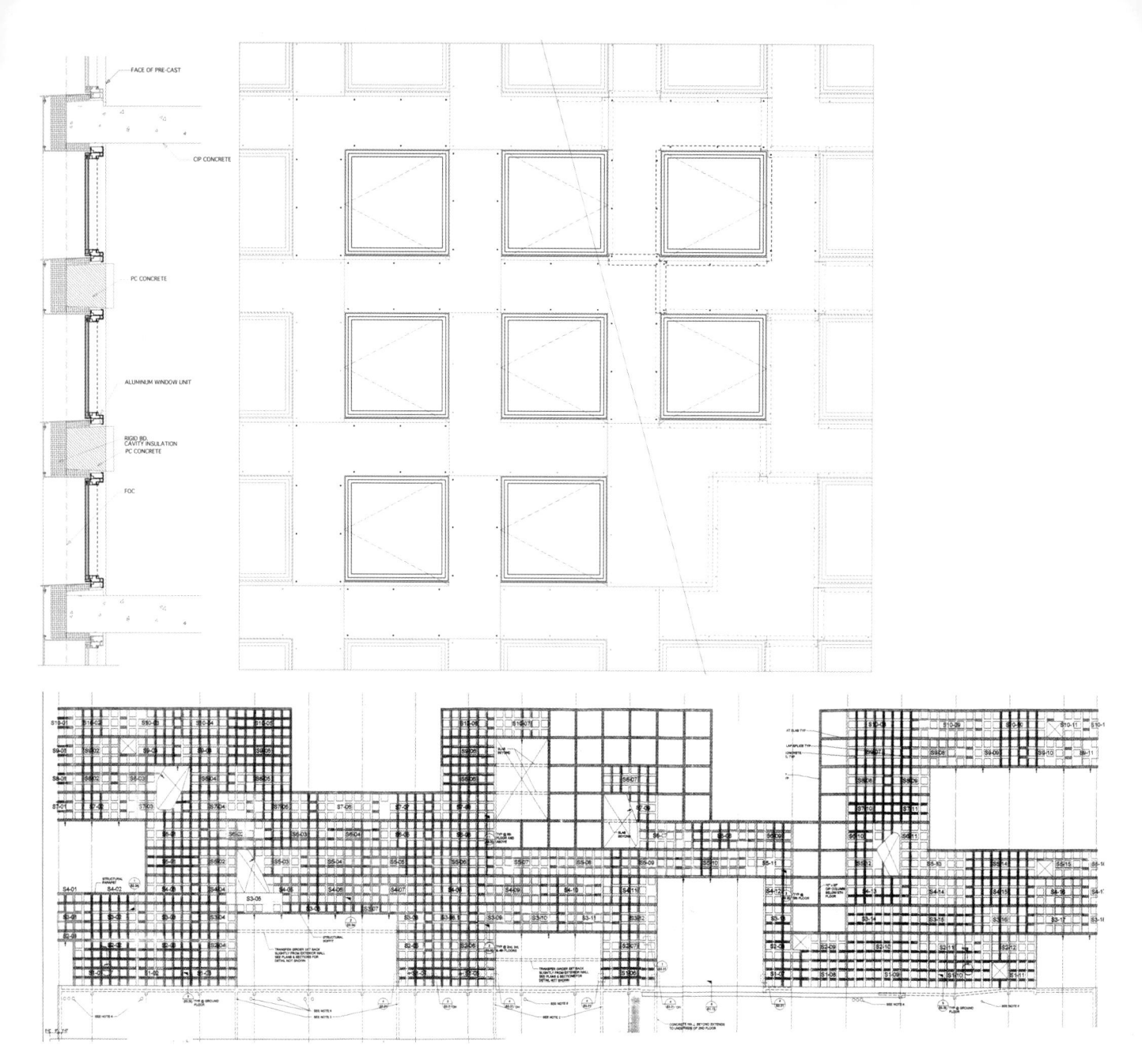

TOP: Typical wall section and partial elevation
BOTTOM: Structural diagram, south elevation
showing color-coded window jambs

opposite:
Color-coded window jambs, detail

COLORED WINDOW JAMBS

Based upon a structural diagram used to coordinate the size of reinforcing steel in the Perfcon panels, the colored jambs express the anticipated maximum stresses in the structure. The colors reveal the size of the reinforcing steel cast within the Perfcon Panels. Blue=#5, Green=#6, Yellow=#7, Orange=#8, Red=#9 and #10. Uncolored areas are #5 or smaller.

Student room with custom porous furniture

STUDENT ROOMS

SH: Each room at Simmons Hall has its own bath. The program called for 50 percent single rooms and 50 percent doubles, each with its own bath. In terms of size, the building is comparable to Aalto's Baker House, but a major difference—to my mind an improvement—is that we provide a dimension of 9 feet 2 inches from floor to ceiling. This dimension derives from the nine-square window pattern found inside each room. To provide views out for both seated and standing occupants, we determined 26-inch window openings. We used the proportions of the Golden Section to tune the dimensions of the room, resulting in the very generous vertical dimension. In effect, the rooms are like mini lofts. A typical dorm—even Baker House did this—provides only 8 feet of ceiling, and that additional 14 inches makes a huge difference. It allows the possibility of elevating the bed and maintaining a comfortable height above and below.

TG: **Was there resistance to the increased ceiling height?**

SH: Again, I believe we benefited from the compressed timetable. By the time we entered the cost-shaving process, it was too late for such a radical change as modifying the floor-to-floor heights. It would have impacted every element and system in the building. But that additional space is, I think, crucial to the quality of the rooms. It is a very precious 14 inches.

Also, all of the windows are operable, so the air movement in the building is tremendous. I was there recently when the temperature outside was 95 degrees. But up on the eighth floor, there was a perfect breeze moving through the space.

TG: **The building is not air-conditioned, is it?**

SH: It has a special HVAC system called a Puff System. On the hottest days of the year, there is

ABOVE and OPPOSITE: Computer renderings of student
rooms with custom porous furniture

80   STUDENT ROOMS

STUDENT ROOMS 81

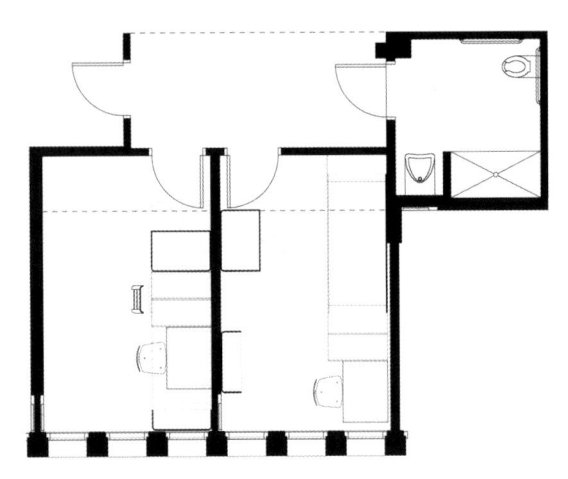

Single room, floor plan

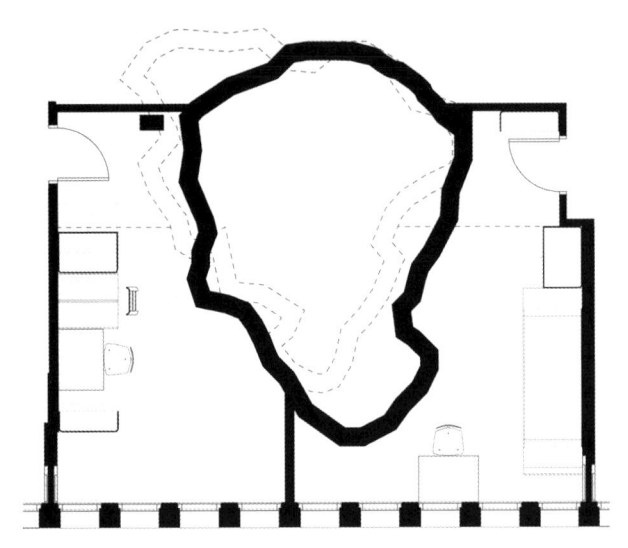

Single room with atrium wall, floor plan

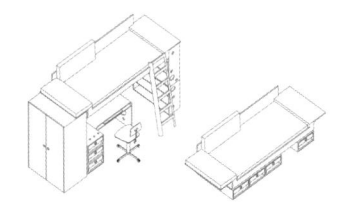

Single-room furniture

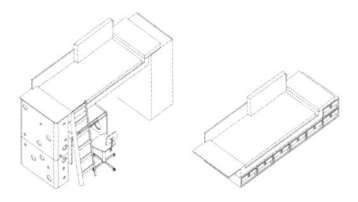

Single-room furniture

82 STUDENT ROOMS

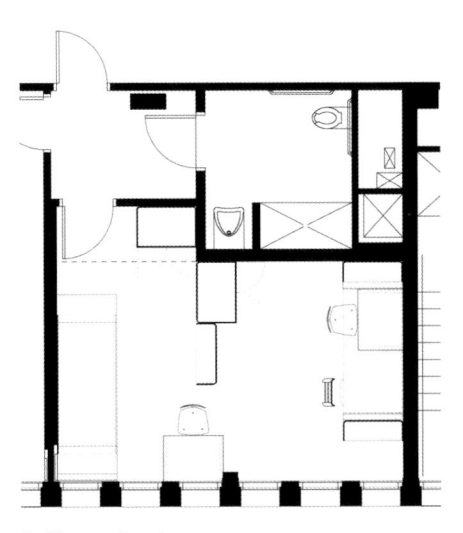

Double room, floor plan

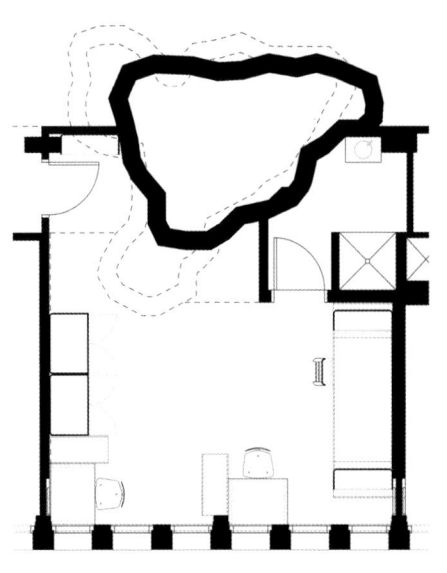

Double room with atrium, floor plan

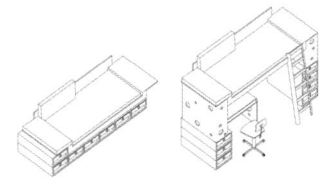

Double-room furniture

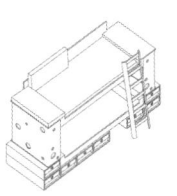

Double-room furniture

STUDENT ROOMS

TOP LEFT: Student lounge
CENTER LEFT: Auditorium
BOTTOM LEFT: Corridor

TOP RIGHT: Student lounge
CENTER RIGHT: Lobby
BOTTOM RIGHT: Student lounge

supplemental cooling; but you are correct, cooling is primarily passive. With the Puff System, you might say it is about 15 percent air-conditioned.

FURNITURE

TG: **Your office designed most of the furniture for the building. Tell us about that.**

SH: We designed the furniture for the student rooms as a series of interchangeable components that would allow maximum flexibility. We set the dimensions such that beds could be elevated or down at the floor; in each case they would line up with the windows properly. A series of playful perforations in the wood panels brought in the idea of porosity.

Also, furniture in a dormitory setting tends to really take a beating, and the wood components should weather well. Plastic furniture does not look very good after it has been nicked and dinged, but wood has the capacity to absorb more abuse; it has an aging capacity. Unlike plastic, it can be refinished periodically, as has been done with Aalto's wood furniture in Baker House.

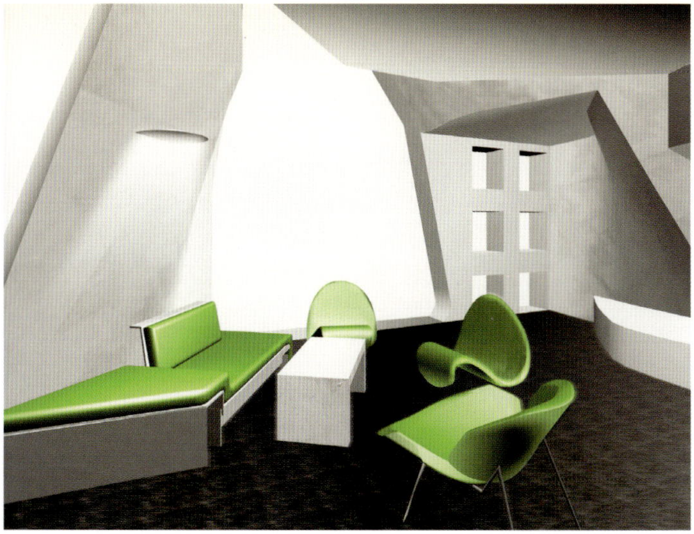
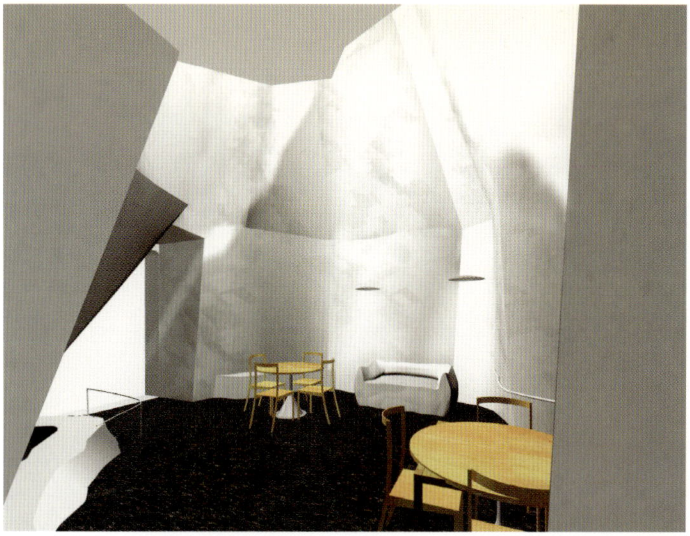
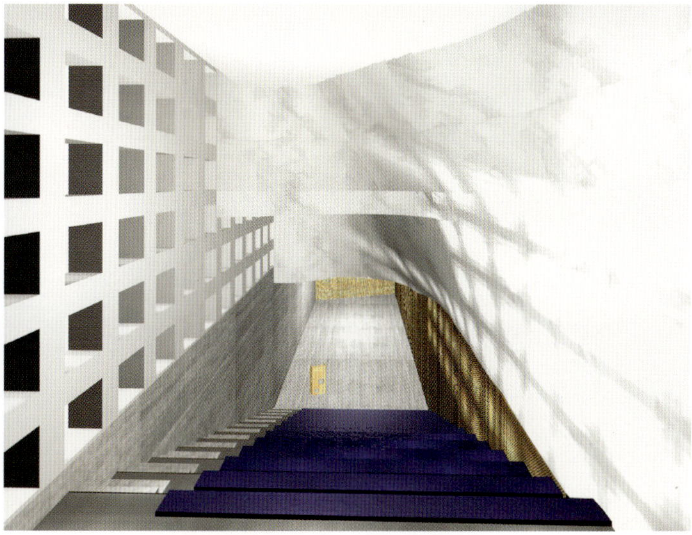
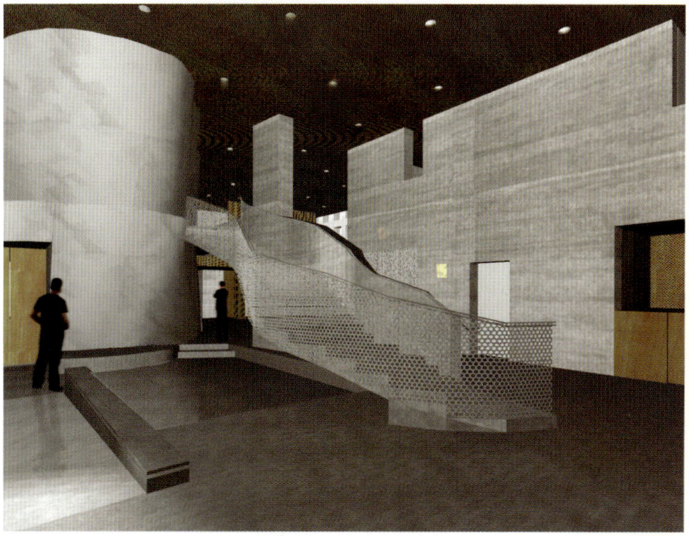
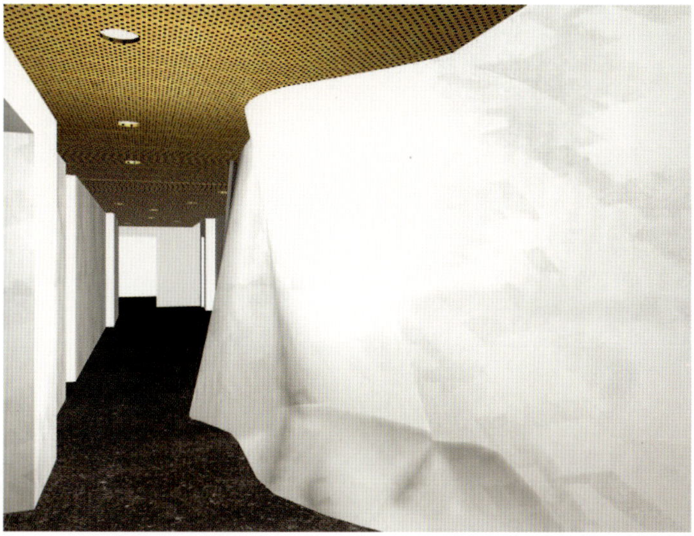
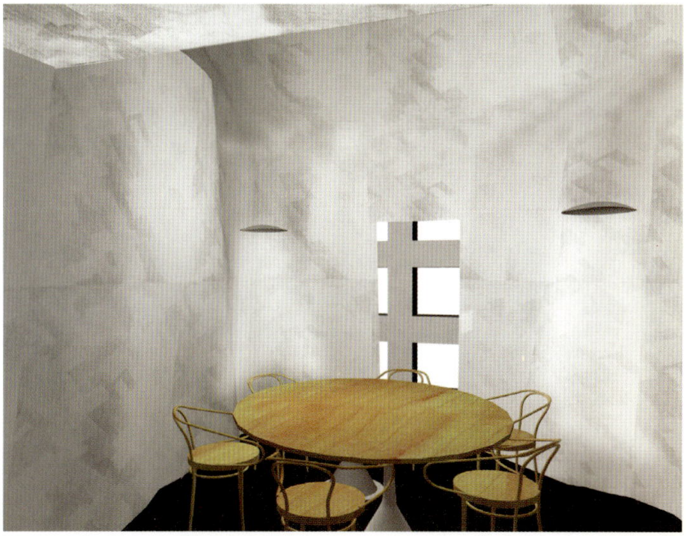

Dining area

86 FURNITURE

Mailbox and student lounge

FLOOR PLANS

Second-floor plan

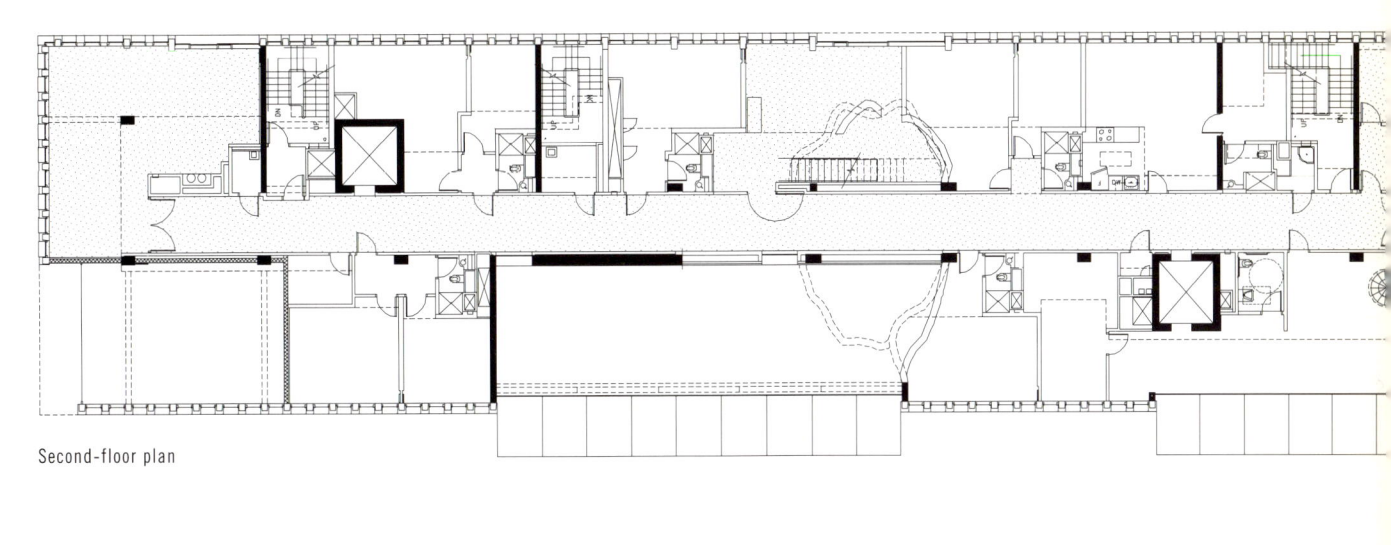

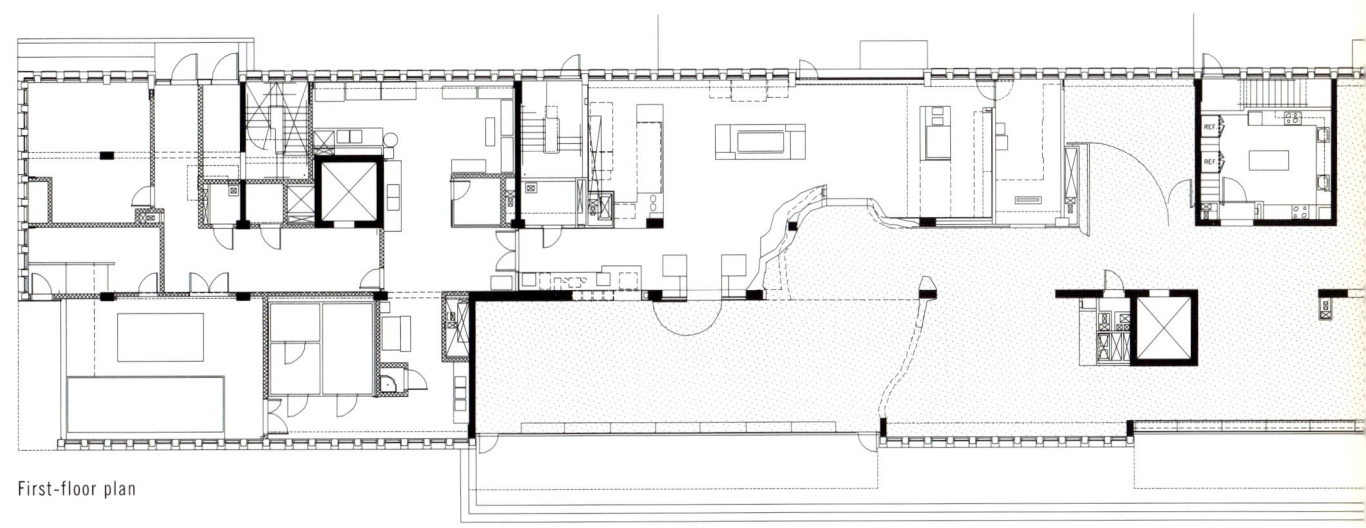

First-floor plan

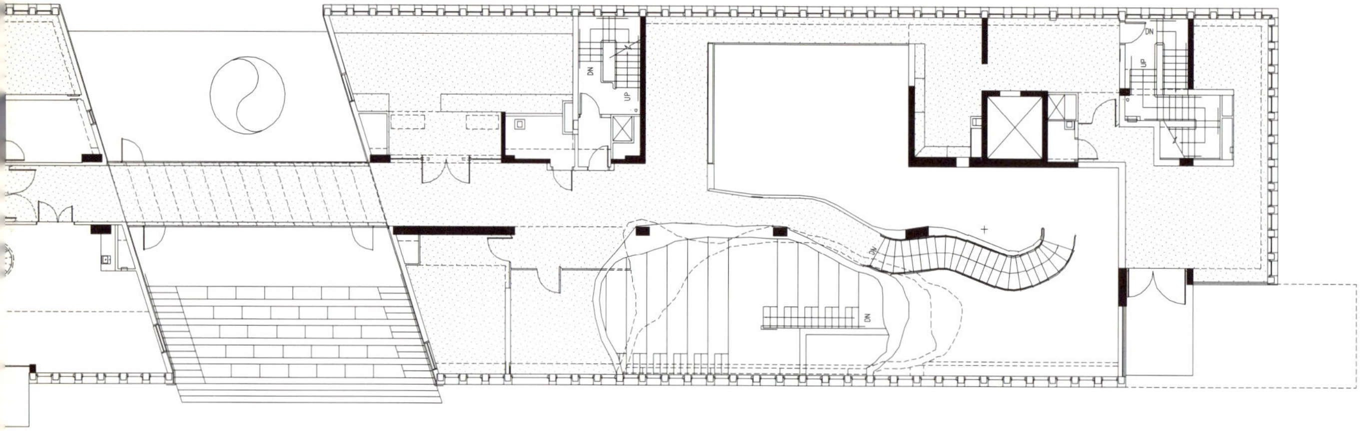

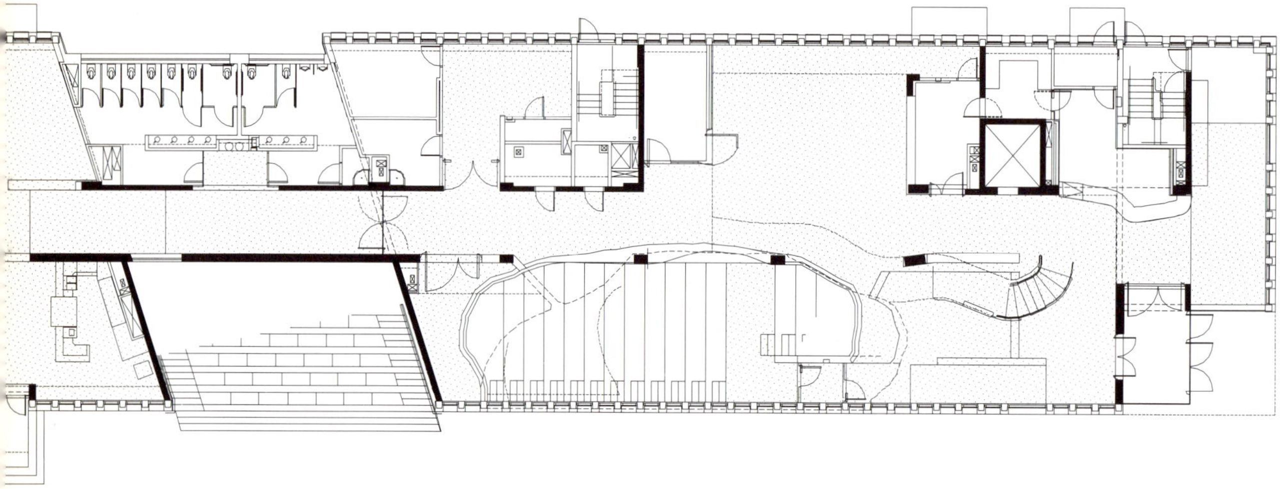

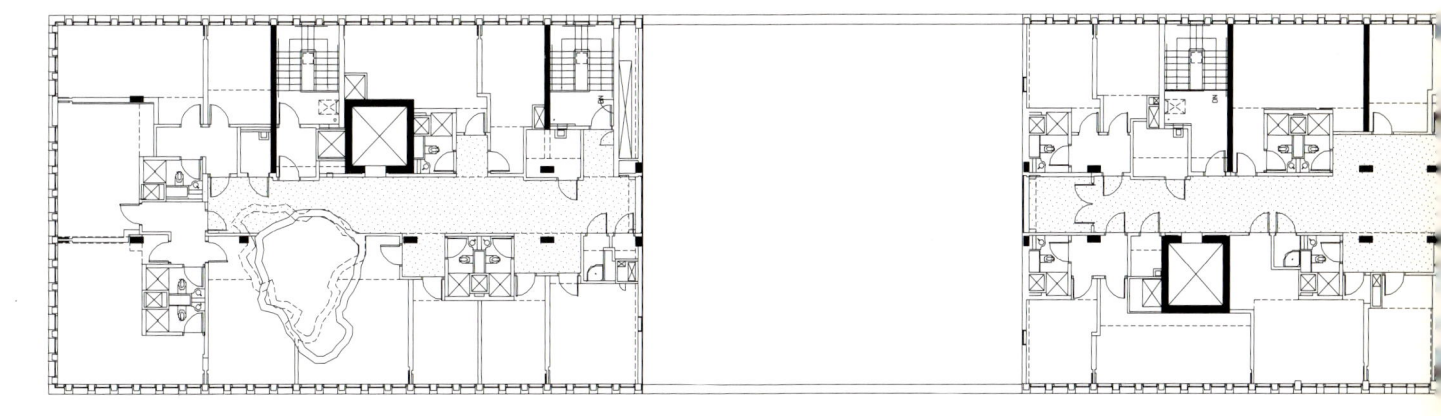

Tenth-floor plan

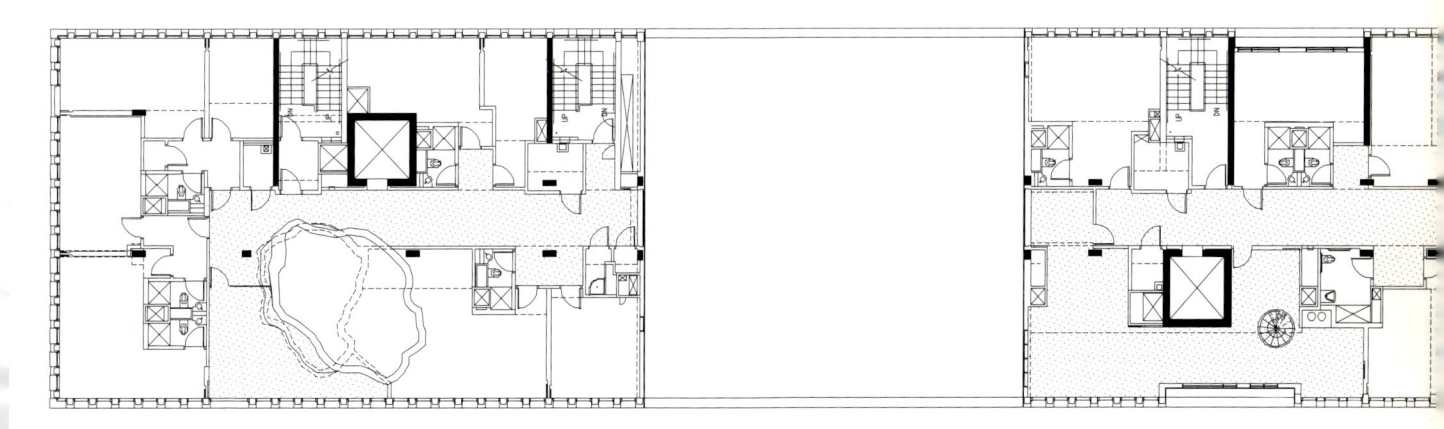

Ninth-floor plan

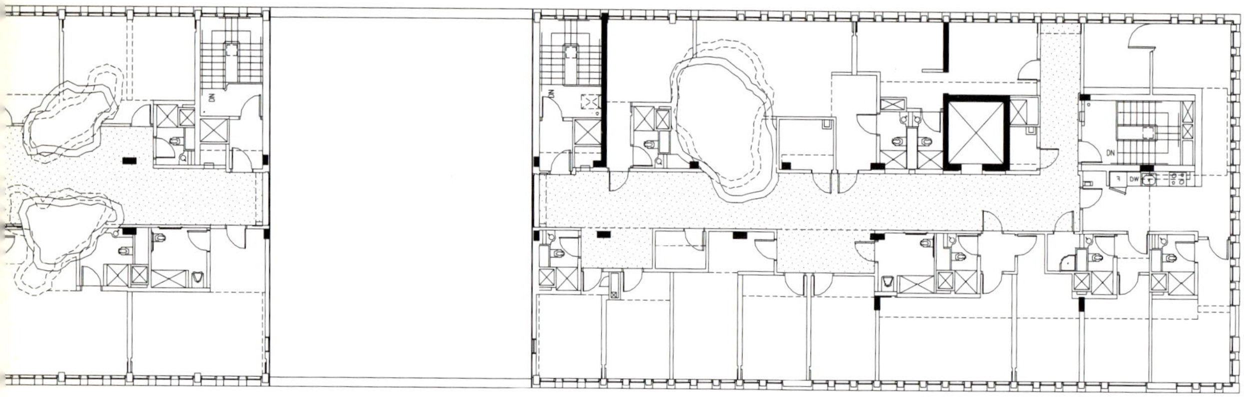

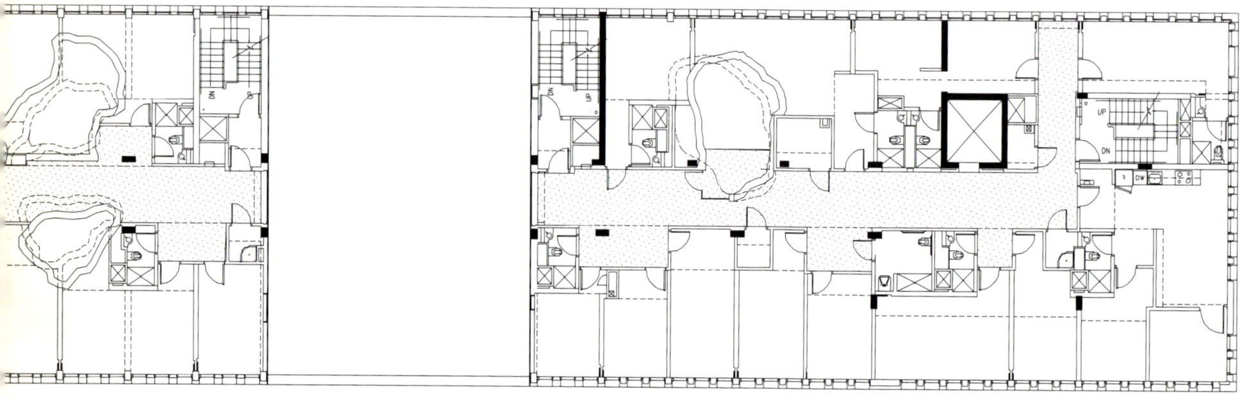

EXECUTION

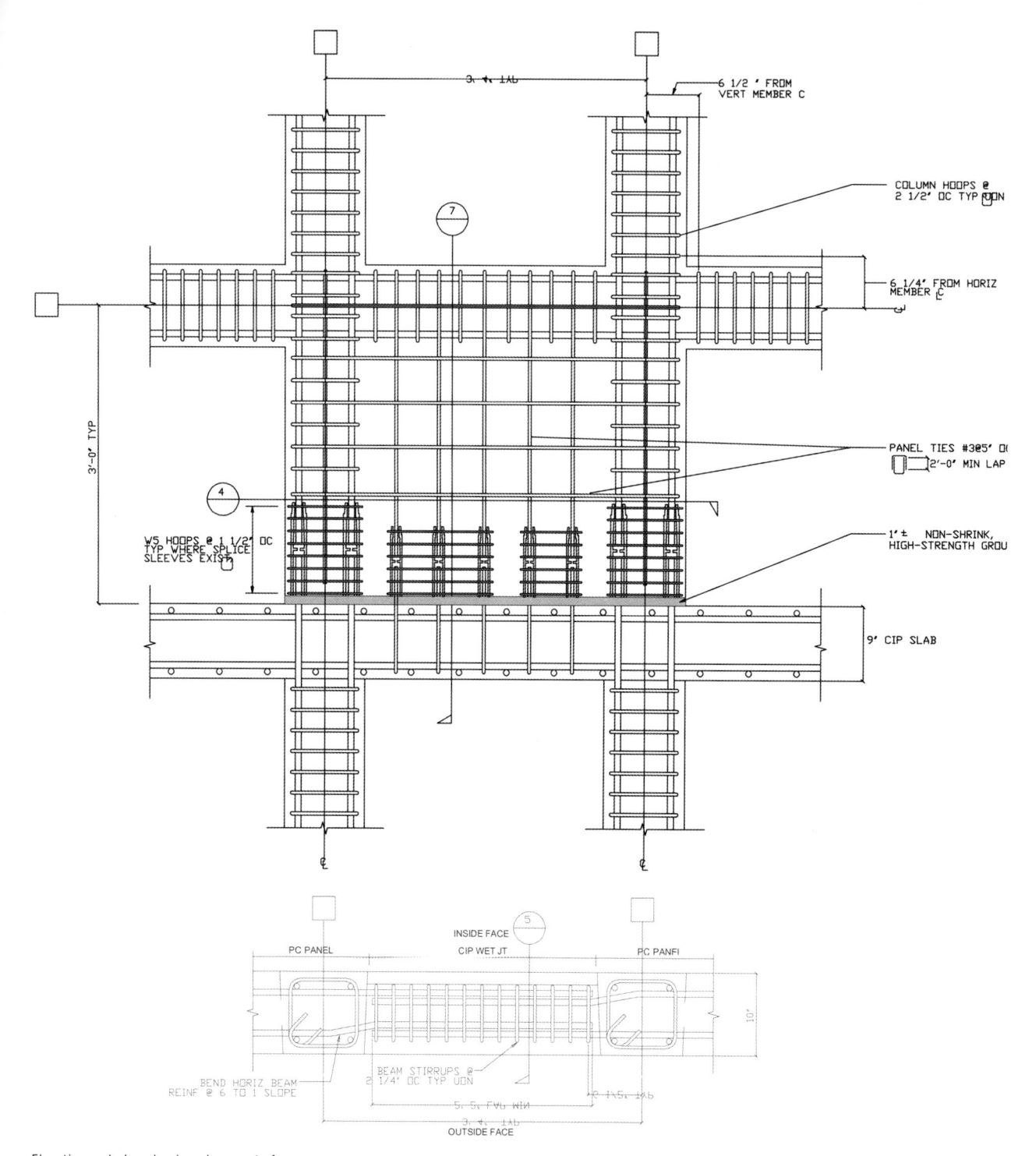

Elevation and plan showing placement of reinforcement in Perfcon panels

EXECUTION

TG: One of the great strengths I see in the building is its ability to create a lot of difference within a very regular system. Each of the ten houses within the building, through its individual lounge space but also through its relationship to the other houses, to exterior views, to the street, etc., takes on its own personality. Also, the crenellated form of the building makes the interior spaces feel much more compact. As a result, one never finds him- or herself in a 300-foot hallway—the cutouts radically change the way a large double-loaded corridor building operates.

SH: The building has been completed for a while, and there has been a critical response. Certain more conservative critics hate the voids, referring to them as "smoke signals" or "gray goo." But the response from the students has been completely the opposite. They live in these spaces and get to experience the way the building reveals itself, as in the ways that you describe.

TG: **How do you respond to your critics?**

SH: I take a certain enjoyment from reading this cantankerous criticism, but most of it has very little effect on me. The fact of the matter is that the building aspires to a feeling of joy. I hope it has the same kind of joy that a young person feels when he or she is involved in something creatively, that moment when the imagination takes flight. I hope that my work and my teaching can bring that kind of joy into architecture as well.

JK: **I do not think it is possible to be successful in architecture—in any field for that matter—unless the things you think about are not simply knowledge but are actually joy. If one does not feel joy in the structure of the city, or in the difference between columns and pilotis, then just forget it.**

Fabrication of Perfcon panels

opposite:
TOP: Selected panel elevations
BOTTOM: Panel reinforcing details

N1-06 N1-05 N1-04 N1-02 S6-07

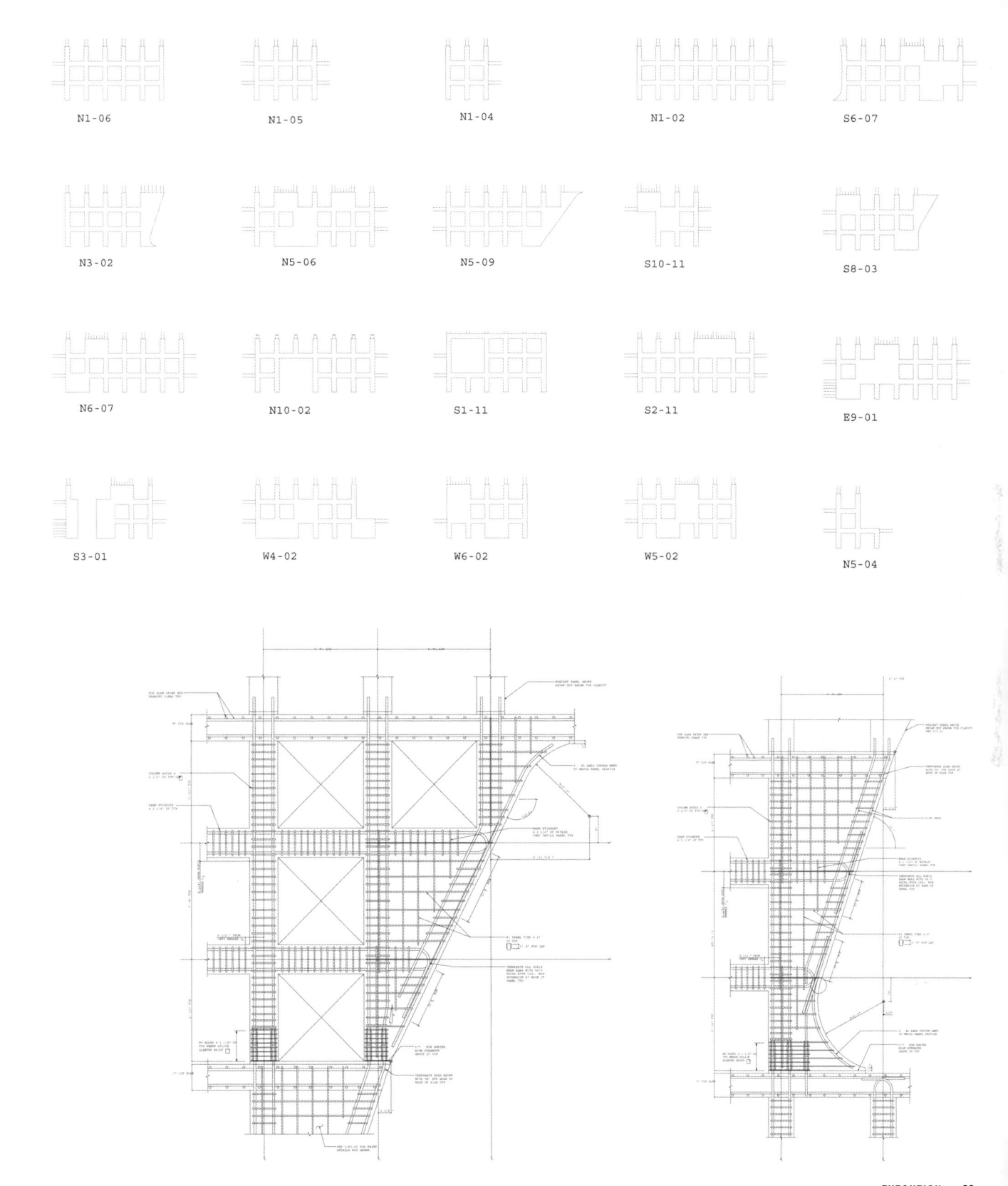

N3-02 N5-06 N5-09 S10-11 S8-03

N6-07 N10-02 S1-11 S2-11 E9-01

S3-01 W4-02 W6-02 W5-02 N5-04

EXECUTION 99

ABOVE and OPPOSITE: Delivery and installation of Perfcon panels

SH: You are right. But with that joy often comes pain. Making architecture brings to me exactly this kind of joy you are talking about, but when you have something unresolved on the drawing board, when a design is not going well, it just tears you apart. You can't sleep, you can't eat—it's that serious. This, I think, is the danger of having too many projects. Unless you become cynical and blasé, you just come apart at the seams. In the '70s, I wanted to work for Louis Kahn. One of his associates told me that Kahn had such enormous energy because he did not build anything until he was fifty. Lou was a child at fifty, wonderfully naïve and not worn down by the system. Because of this, he could really build. His childlike wonder at the power of architecture helped him to convince his clients to get behind his ideas.

TG: **Your master plan proposed a series of buildings, thematically related but formally diverse, creating a definite but porous edge along Vassar Street. Will that plan go forward? Have your ideas of porosity been adopted?**

SH: I hope so. Larry Bacow has left MIT to become the president of Tufts University. Also, the economic bubble burst, so who knows?

TG: **In its present context, Simmons Hall is not part of an edge but rather a distinct object. Does the current condition detract from the way you intended the building to be received?**

SH: Certainly the original vision proposed something much more extensive, but I don't think that the intensity of the architecture is lessened. Whatever the concept of the design, I feel it should have a range of aspirations. It should operate at the level of the building, the level of the detail, the level of the city. Of course we would like to pursue the idea on as many levels as possible, to have it resonate throughout the campus,

100 EXECUTION

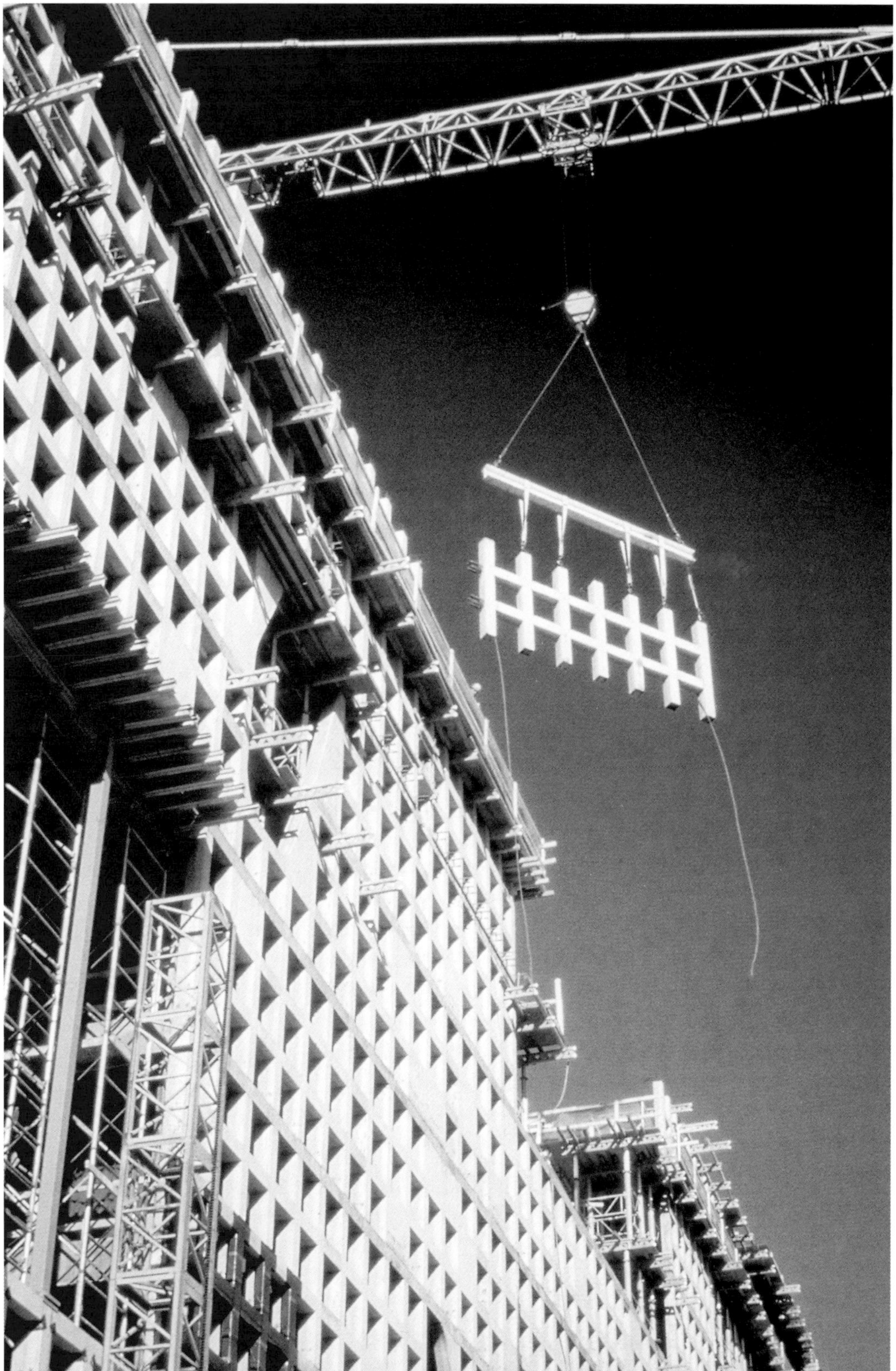

into the city of Cambridge. Sadly, this is not always possible.

I would like to build another building on Vassar Street. It would be a totally different building based on the idea of porosity. I did a design for a pocket park at the building entry, but it was eliminated.

JK: **Was it designed in terms of the concept of the building?**

SH: Yes. I was thinking about stone as a porous material. The whole thing was to be executed in yellow plantings and blue stone. In a sense, I was taking the typical green color of a park and breaking it down to its primary components. I was thinking about the concept of the building at another scale and in another material, themes and variations. I could take that concept and just keep going.

But that raises a real conceptual dilemma. Maybe I shouldn't keep going. I had a conversation with Eric Walker recently. He told me that each of my projects derives from a very individual set of concepts and circumstances, making each one seem like a one-off. Then he asked, "why not do a series?" That is a very irritating critical remark about my work, but perhaps there is something true about it. I am primarily interested in pursuing new ideas with each project, but there is in my work what I would call a discontinuous series.

JK: **Stendhal said that an author can only write one book, no matter how many times he writes it. Your existential condition guarantees a continuity to the work, but that is different from pursuing a serial problem, in the manner of, say, Josef Albers.**

SH: I am not interested in pursuing a serial problem.

JK: **Nonetheless, you have developed a style, a way of working that can be traced back to your**

Installation of aluminum window panels

LEFT: Details of Perfcon panels at large-scale opening
RIGHT: Breaks in the Perfcon grid occur where interior sponge spaces intersect with the exterior wall

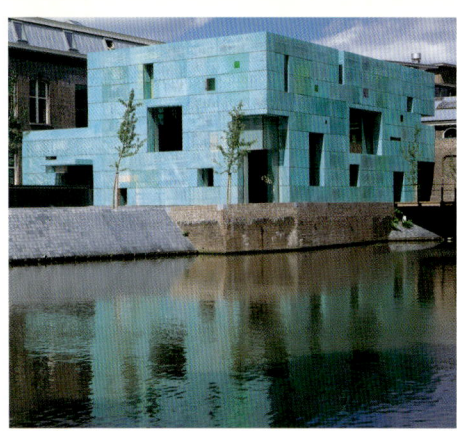

LEFT: Sarphatistraat offices,
Amsterdam, The Netherlands,
1996–2000
RIGHT: Menger sponge

earliest projects. **I would say that by the time of the Gymnasium-Bridge project, you had established that style.**

SH: I would like to get out of it then.

JK: **I do not mean this in a derogatory way. Beethoven had a style, but none of his symphonies sounds like another. It simply means there is an integrity to the work, an integrity that comes through no matter how the concepts are framed. It does not matter if you want it or not, you cannot avoid it.**

SH: In each of my projects, there is a very distinct conceptual strategy. For example, the Sarphatistraat Building in Amsterdam was based on two concepts: "Patterns in a Chromatic Field," by the composer Morton Feldman, and a Menger sponge. One might say that the idea of porosity at MIT came from Sarphatistraat, and it is true that the buildings share certain affinities, but I would argue that, in the end, these are two very different buildings.

I am not interested in becoming the kind of artist that produces an entire body of work in a serialized way, always working with the same parameters. To me that is the opposite of interesting.

EXECUTION 105

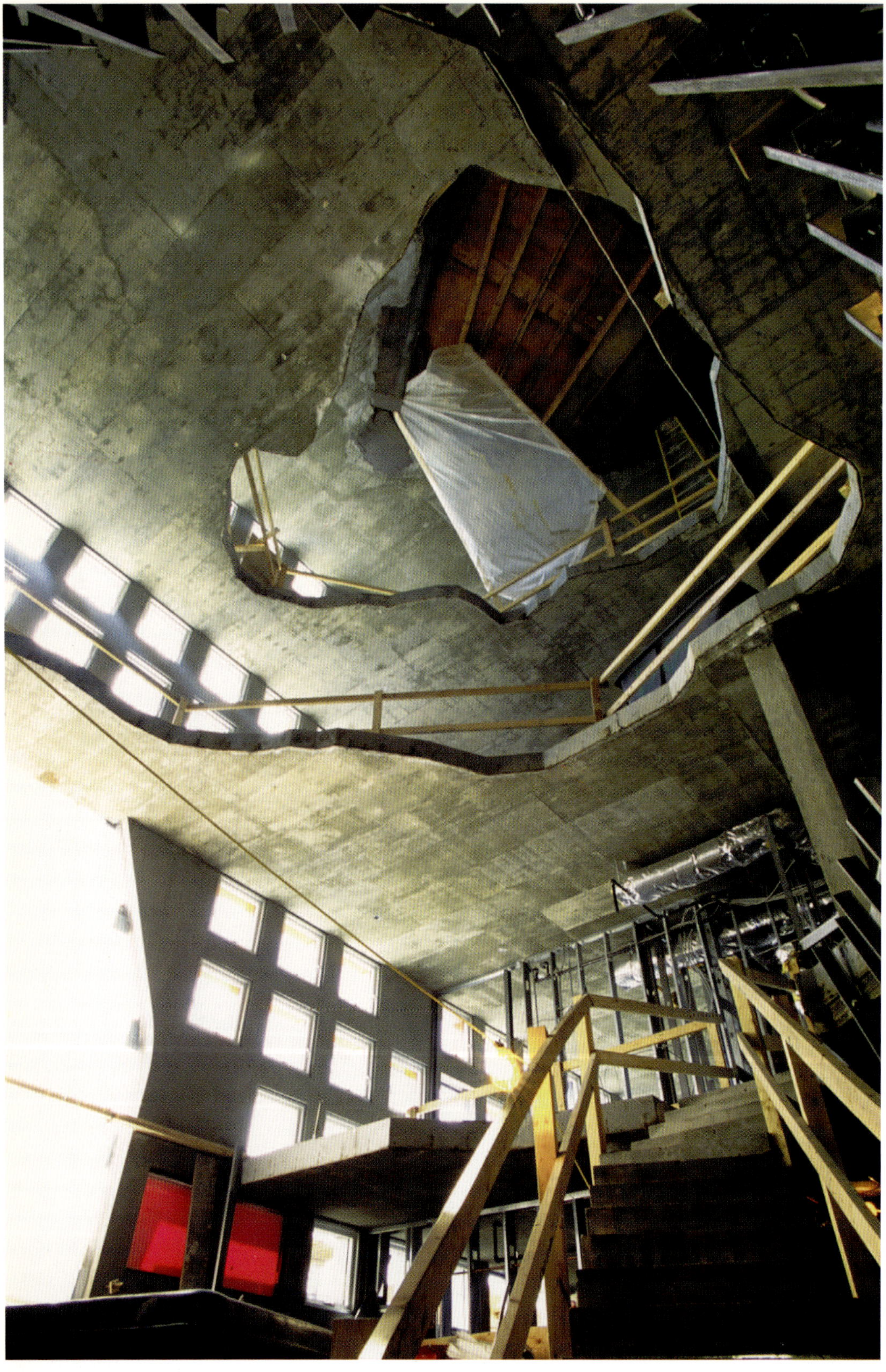

Construction of the ruled surface that forms the sponge spaces

opposite:
Construction of floor slabs with openings for sponge space

JK: **At MIT, one of the great successes of Simmons Hall is that you understand that its occupants are temporary; it is not a model of how to live forever.**

SH: No, not at all. It is an experience for at most four years.

JK: **Now Baker House, on the other hand...**

SH: I don't think Baker House is a model of how to live forever.

JK: **Aalto understood that it would be a temporary place to live but his ideas were more idealized. You seem more concerned with immediate experience.**

SH: The project for Simmons Hall forced me to reckon with Aalto's work from the beginning. Early in the project, Larry Bacow said to me, "We are giving you the same program as Baker House. Make a better building." That is a tough charge.

JK: **A better building architecturally or a better place to live? For me these are two very different things.**

SH: For Larry, it was certainly about making a better place to live. But in my mind, as with all my projects, it also has to be about the architecture.

JK: **Simmons Hall is a curious building for me. I am trying to figure out what it has to do to perform architecturally.**

SH: It has to be an inspired place for the students to live in a one year, day-to-day existence at one of the most high-pressure universities in the country. One thing I think this building ought to do is distract them. It should playfully nudge them into thinking about something other than the problems with their studies. Occasionally, they might feel a little joy, a little offhandedness, in their daily lives.

I wanted to make a building that would not be taken for granted. It should engage its occupants,

LEFT: Lobby under construction
RIGHT: Dining area under construction

should become a part of their lives. Its calling is more than just the problem of a dormitory—you know, fresh air, good ventilation, whatever. It should certainly accommodate those things, and accommodate them well, but to be a work of architecture, it has to be more than that. I am most concerned with that emotional and spiritual component that is never part of the program. That is the most difficult and most important part.

JK: **What you are describing makes the measure of the building how well it performs for its occupant. I am trying to figure out what I would teach about this building. What does it do that might make us think differently, not simply about the problem of living in a dormitory for a year, but about the problem of architecture?**

Take the punched windows. In their scale, in their materiality, I am able to understand them as belonging to a specific tradition in architecture that does not refer outside of the discipline. But this is not the case with the informal cuts, whether in their appearance on the facades or as forms and spaces within the building. In each case, they refer outside themselves—they are an architectural paraphrase of the sponge. What I would like to figure out is how to take these kinds of forms out of their referential role, to make them, in their essence, architectural rather than representational.

SH: Look out the window to New York City. With almost every building in view, you can tell how many floors they have. The breakthrough of Simmons Hall is that because the thickness of the floors is exactly the thickness of the structure, everything is equal. There is no way of telling how many floors there are. Suddenly, that does something. It does something in relation to other buildings around it, it does something in relation to the history of architecture. It becomes without scale.

Main staircase in lobby under construction

EXECUTION 109

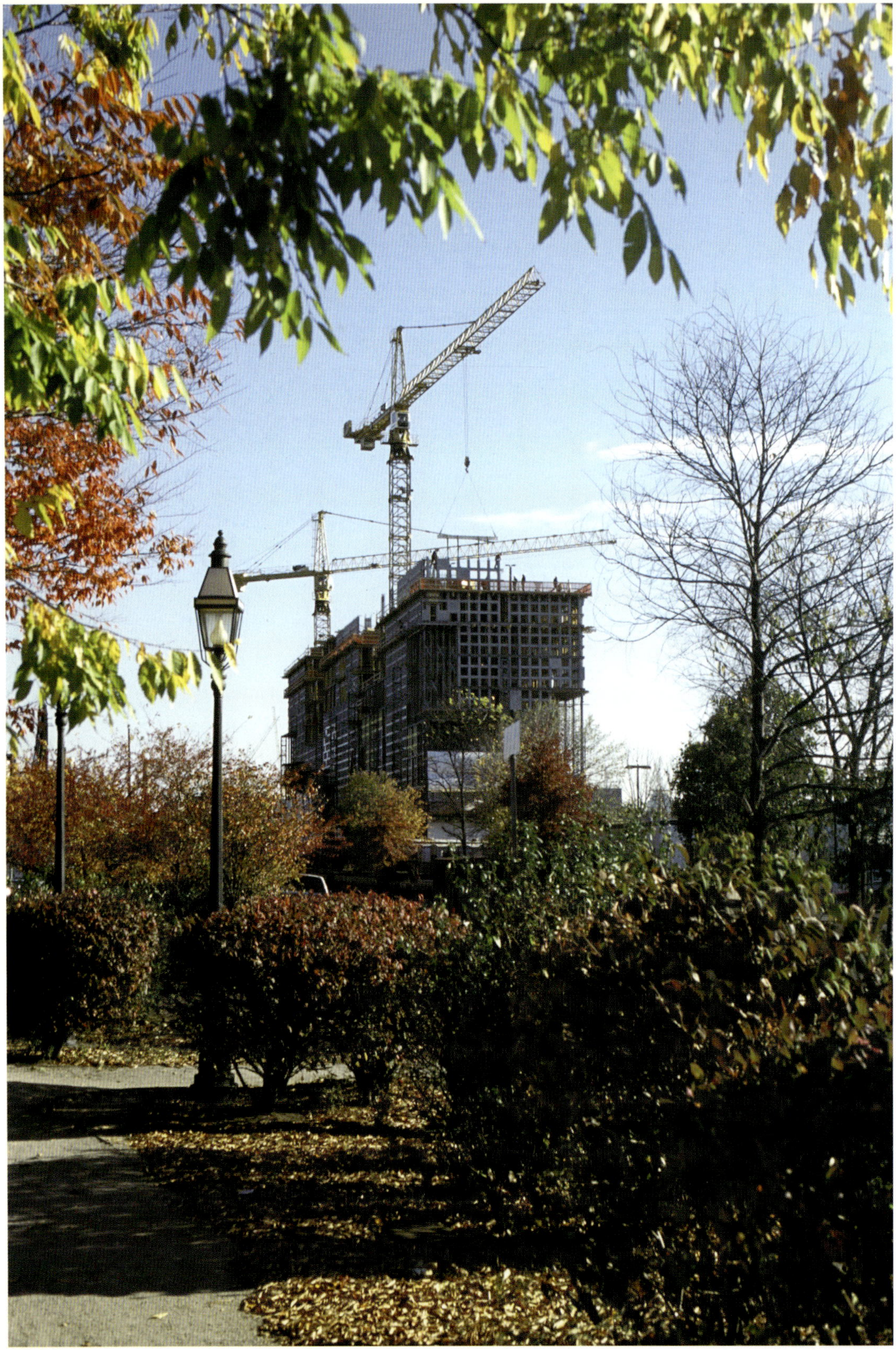

View of construction from campus

opposite:
View of construction from Briggs Field

JK: **That is the most important effect of the building. But when you introduce the informal cuts, the question of scale specificity returns.**

SH: Except that you cannot be sure. You cannot know whether the cuts happen on floors or across floors.

JK: **I would say that the building's lack of contextuality and its scalelessness are its greatest achievements. But when you introduce the sponge holes, you run into a conflict between these two types of openings.**

I am only interested in the architectural problems that buildings pose to be solved. I think this building is an argument about a new understanding of collectivity, of provisionality, of the monolithic. It deals with the problem of difference within these conditions. It takes a large architectural vocabulary to work these problems out, and in this case, some of it works, and some of it doesn't.

What would need to happen to make the argument you are making coalesce into something that is wholly architectural? I am not criticizing the building, I am just trying to figure out how you would pursue the problem further. For example, Chopin wrote waltzes. Anyone can dance to them, so making something to dance to was not the problem. The irreducible qualities of music itself were the problem.

SH: Take a simple drawing. There are a million of them out there. But every once in a while, you will find a drawing with an incredibly emotional intensity. maybe it is Giacometti slashing away, or perhaps Matisse making a single line. The difference between those few and the other million is the problem of design, and that, by the way, is why it is impossible to teach design.

JK: **So you are after this sort of emotional intensity in your work?**

SH: Yes. In every building that I have put up, and there have not been so many, the space is the most important component. It is far more important than any reading of the facades. I try to invest my work with a quality that cannot be reconciled with words.

JK: **Over the last twenty years, architects have confused scale with size. One of the achievements of this building is to only be real in its size. It is only as big as when you are there, there are no other scalar cues.**

SH: Yes, it confounds your reading of scale.

JK: **You have found a way to solve a problem that Herzog and de Meuron first posed with the Basel Signal Boxes. Their solution was to build massive, windowless boxes. We now have an element in our palette that can work on the problem of size versus scale in a new way. I am more interested in that than in the problem of making a sponge out of architecture. The crucial problem is getting beyond paraphrase.**

SH: That is a long process.

JK: **There are half a dozen architects out there working on the same problem. In each case, they are trying to figure out how to make a work irreducible. I think you have been working on that problem for a long time. You drew a lot of energy from Merleau-Ponty and his argument about pre-criticality. Merleau-Ponty came closer than anyone to introducing time into phenomenology, which would also introduce the future. But he never solved the problem.**

    You were always as interested in the future as you were in the pre-critical. By introducing the Menger sponge or porosity or any of the other concepts, you were introducing something alien into the system to see if evolution could occur. You were constantly trying to move from the pre-critical to a new condition.

South facade

opposite:
Installation of aluminum facade panels

SH: Ten years ago, I was on a panel discussion. Rafael Moneo raised the point that everyone was dealing with curtain walls, all of the structures were the same. He proposed that the future of architecture would be completely about skins. That idea totally disgusts me. If that is going to be the future of architecture, then I want to do something else. There has to be more to it than that. Simmons Hall is a building that is interested in reconciling a lot of these issues.

In most buildings, structure is about 25 percent of the cost and 30 percent of the material. So if you don't bring structure to bear on whatever it is you are doing as an architect, then I think that somewhere it's not working. It's not reconciled. Le Corbusier always incorporated the structure, as did Kahn, and Mies. I am interested in maintaining an integral relation of the idea through the structure, the space, and the experience.

But you are a critic; you are interested in the argument. I wonder if you are interested in the role of structure. If I had given in, if this were a steel-frame building, if the exterior were merely a skin hung on a frame, would that make any difference to you?

JK: **Not as such. But I am interested in the depth of the effect. As a critic, I am interested in the debate between surface and skin. That debate introduces the problem of the micro-section. If there is a micro-sectional effect, then it is working in the material sense of the skin. If there is not, then the facade is working in the dematerialized sense of the abstracted surface. For an architect to be forced to one side or the other of that very interesting debate by economics is a real concern today.**

This building has a very palpable micro-section effect. That effect gives the building a certain weight but also a kind of weightlessness in a larger sense. That effect would not be there were the building a frame.

But I do not agree with Moneo. If the problem today is how to deal with a curtain wall, because that is the reality of construction, then that is okay with me.

SH: That's not okay with me. That is the division between us.

TG: **What about the color effect?**

SH: The color was something that I wanted from the beginning. At first, I intended to color code the different houses, to make the different houses identifiable from the exterior. But the students were against this, they preferred a certain anonymity. I came back to New York and thought, "Now what are we going to do?" Then I saw this structural diagram of Guy Nordenson's and I thought that is what we'll do. In the end it did not matter what the coding device was. I was most concerned with getting the color within the jamb and the head, not on the facade but within its section.

JK: **And that color introduces the micro-section of the project.**

SH: Exactly. There is no color on the outside of the building; there is no color on the inside. It is only in the thickness of the wall that you will find the color, in that no-man's land between inside and outside. But that color reflects into the rooms, so there is a wash of the colors within. That is what I wanted to achieve.

TG: **And in those effects, the color transcends its representational role. It is no longer a simple index of the reinforcing steel within.**

JK: **It is much better than color-coding the houses.**

SH: You're right. It's much better. I had a desire for a certain phenomenal effect but did not have the technique to achieve it. The circumstances of the project drove me to a better solution than I had originally planned.

TG: **The challenge in your work is always to develop techniques to reconcile the heuristics you introduce.**

SH: I am doing a project now, the Museum of Civilization, in Marseilles. The project is based on embedded spirals, derived from new discoveries in quark plasma. I find ideas in science so much more interesting than ideas in architecture.

TG: **But with the introduction of these outside ideas, the architectural effects have to compete with the representation of the idea. In your earlier work, such as the Gymnasium-Bridge or the Hybrid Building at Seaside, elaborate narratives gave the buildings their distinctive characters. In the later work, many of the conceptual heuristics are derived from science. In my opinion, the best results come not from the original idea but from the architectural scenarios, from the spaces, forms, and effects these ideas generate.**

SH: I've been criticized again and again about my heuristic devices. In some ways, I feel like I shouldn't say what they are anymore.

JK: **I've always thought that about your work. The issue is not the degree to which the building indicates that idea as a paraphrase, but it's the degree to which these ideas open up architectural possibilities.**

Why would anyone care about how good your science is? You are an architect. The world has a pretty good idea of what a good scientist does, but they've got no idea what a good architect does.

Do I think you are a good scientist? Actually, Steve, you are one of the worst I've ever seen. Do I think you are a good architect? I don't know a scientist who could come close.

COMPLETED CONSTRUCTION

118   COMPLETED CONSTRUCTION

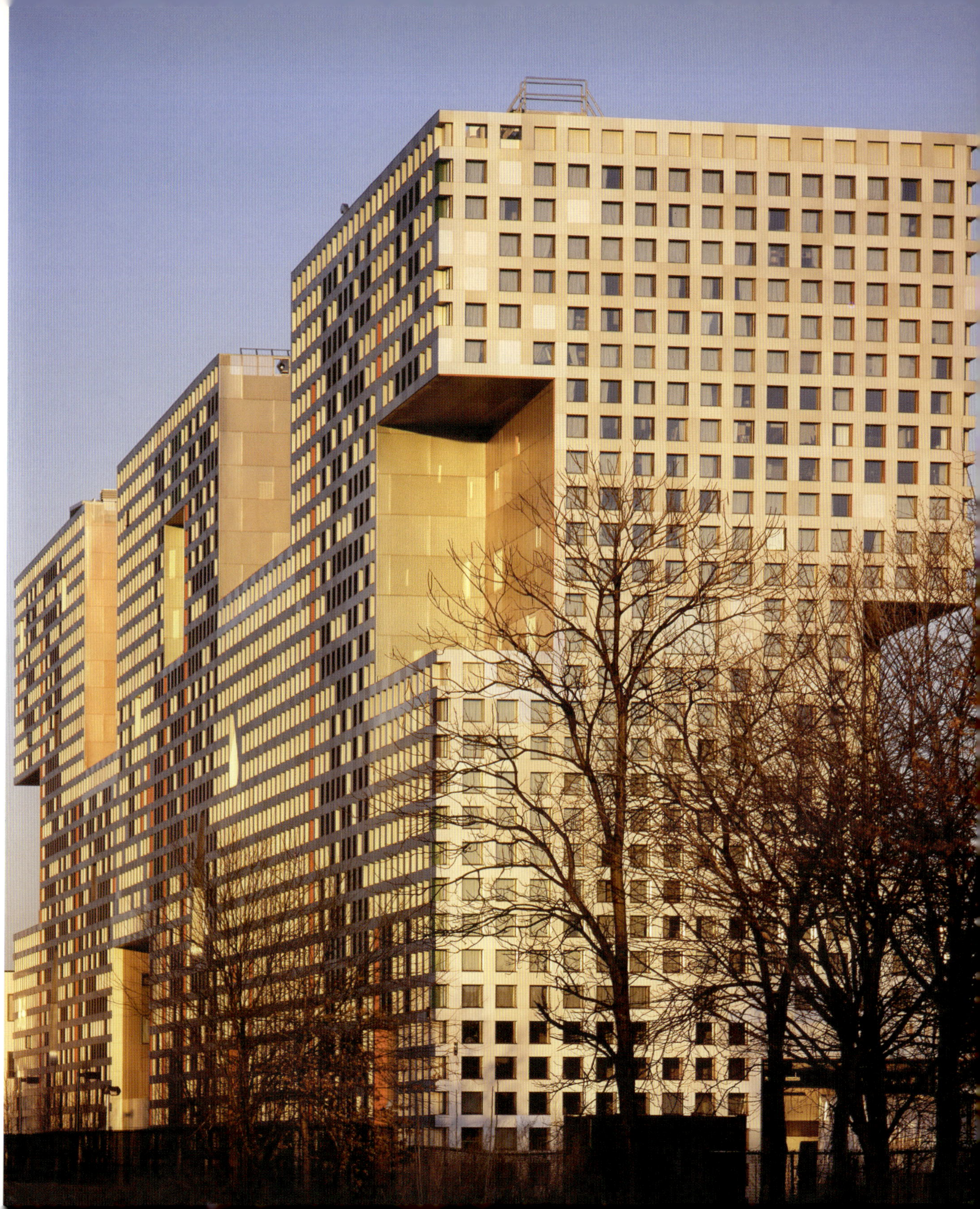

120   COMPLETED CONSTRUCTION

COMPLETED CONSTRUCTION 121

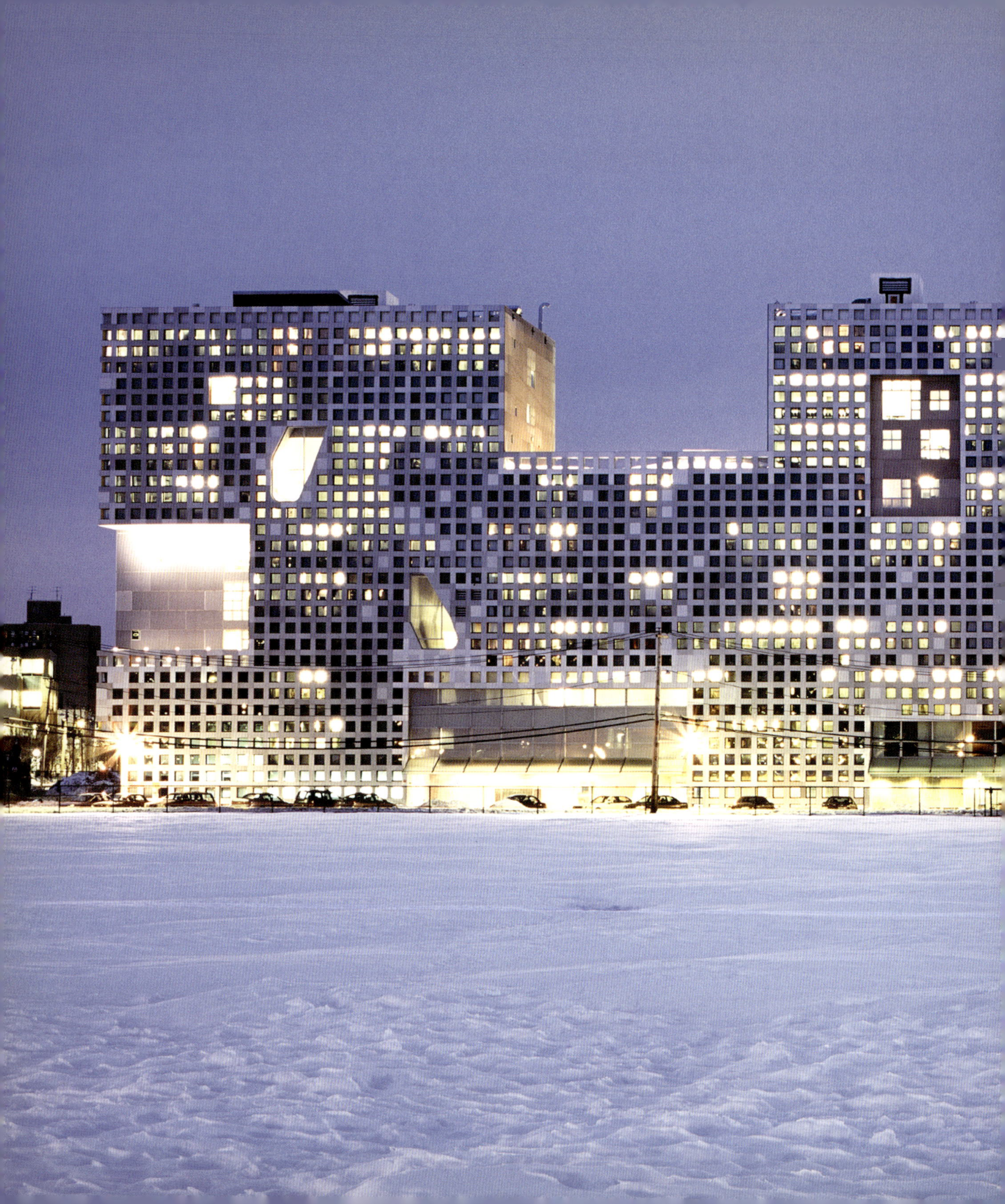

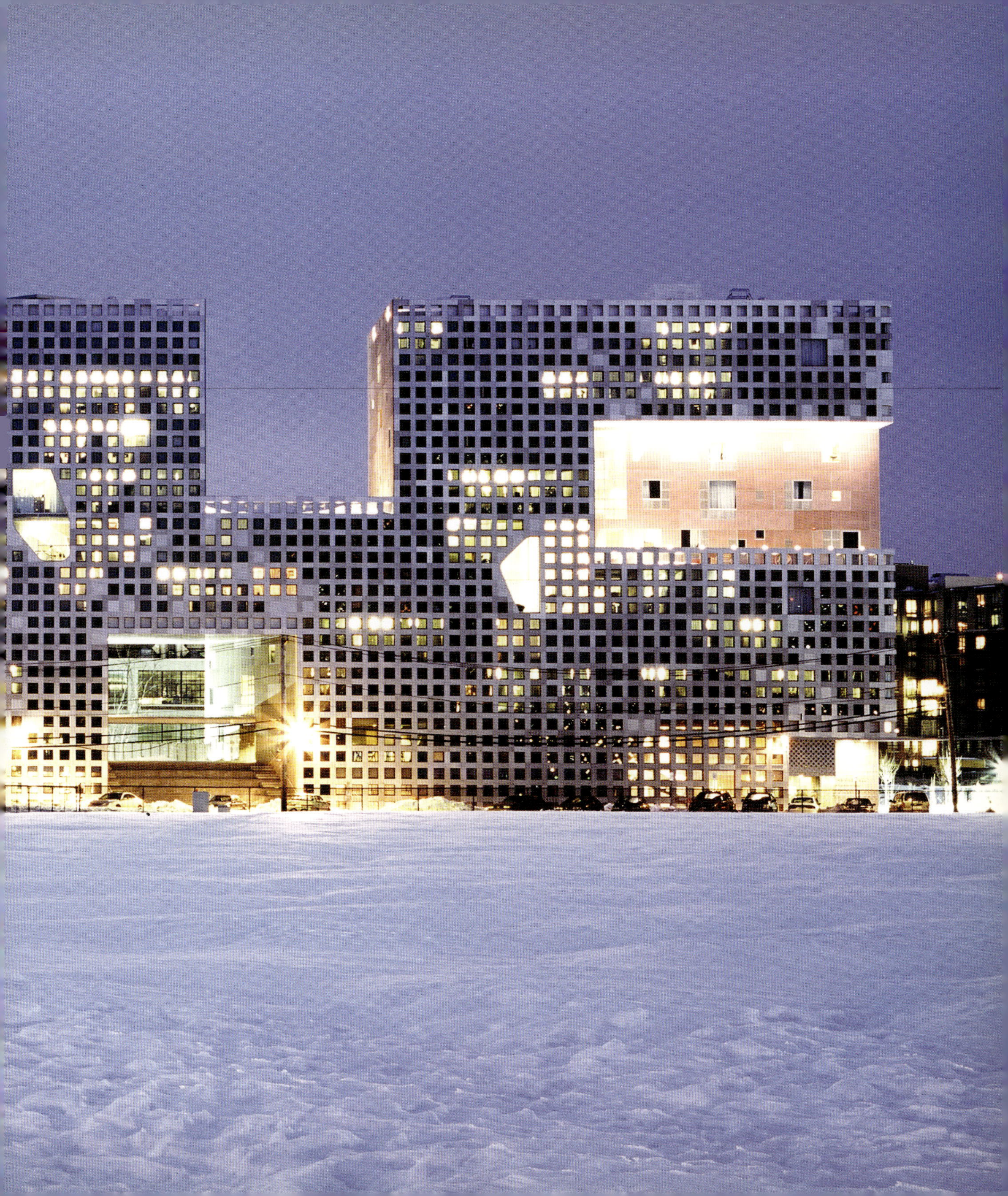

124   COMPLETED CONSTRUCTION

COMPLETED CONSTRUCTION 125

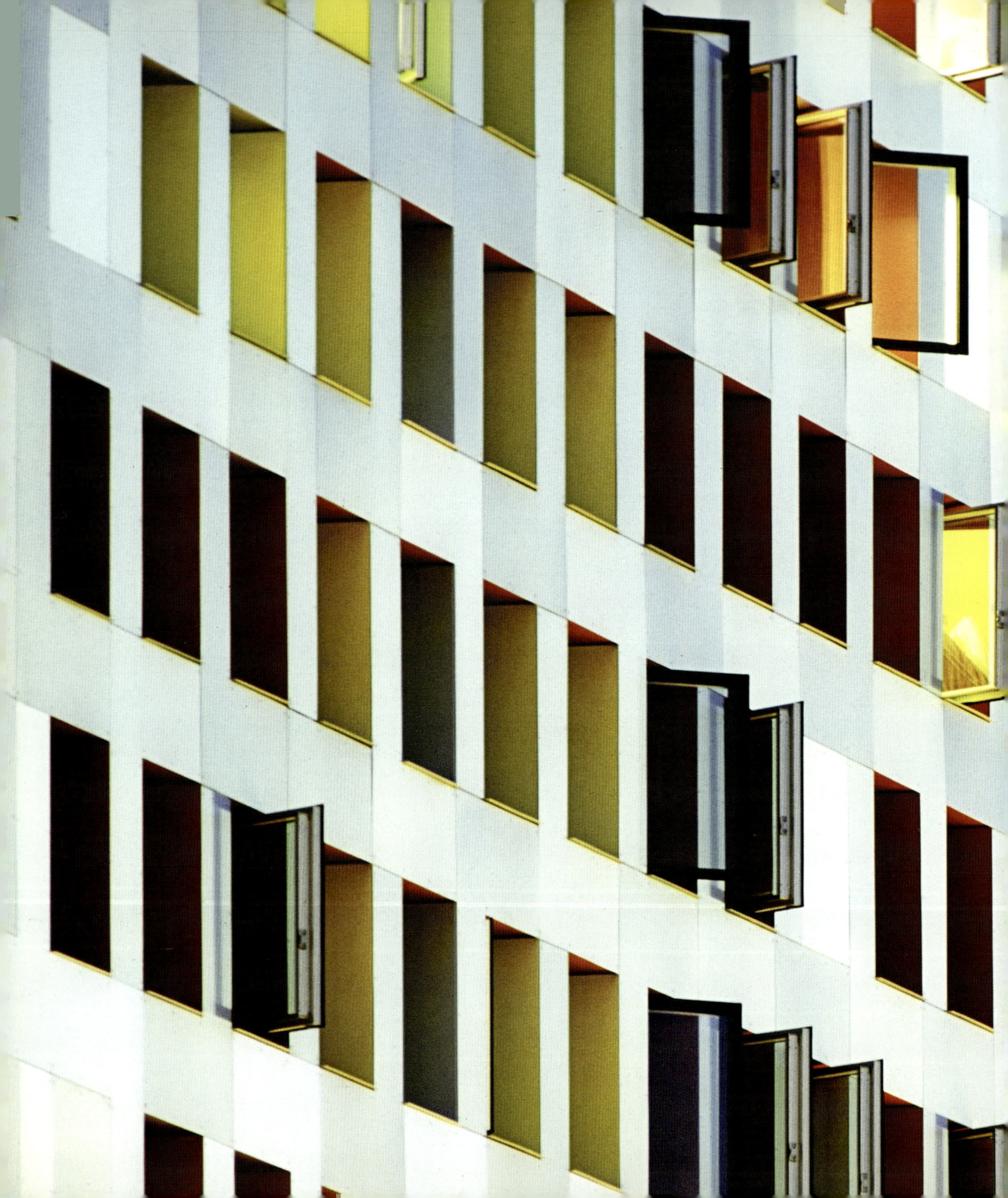

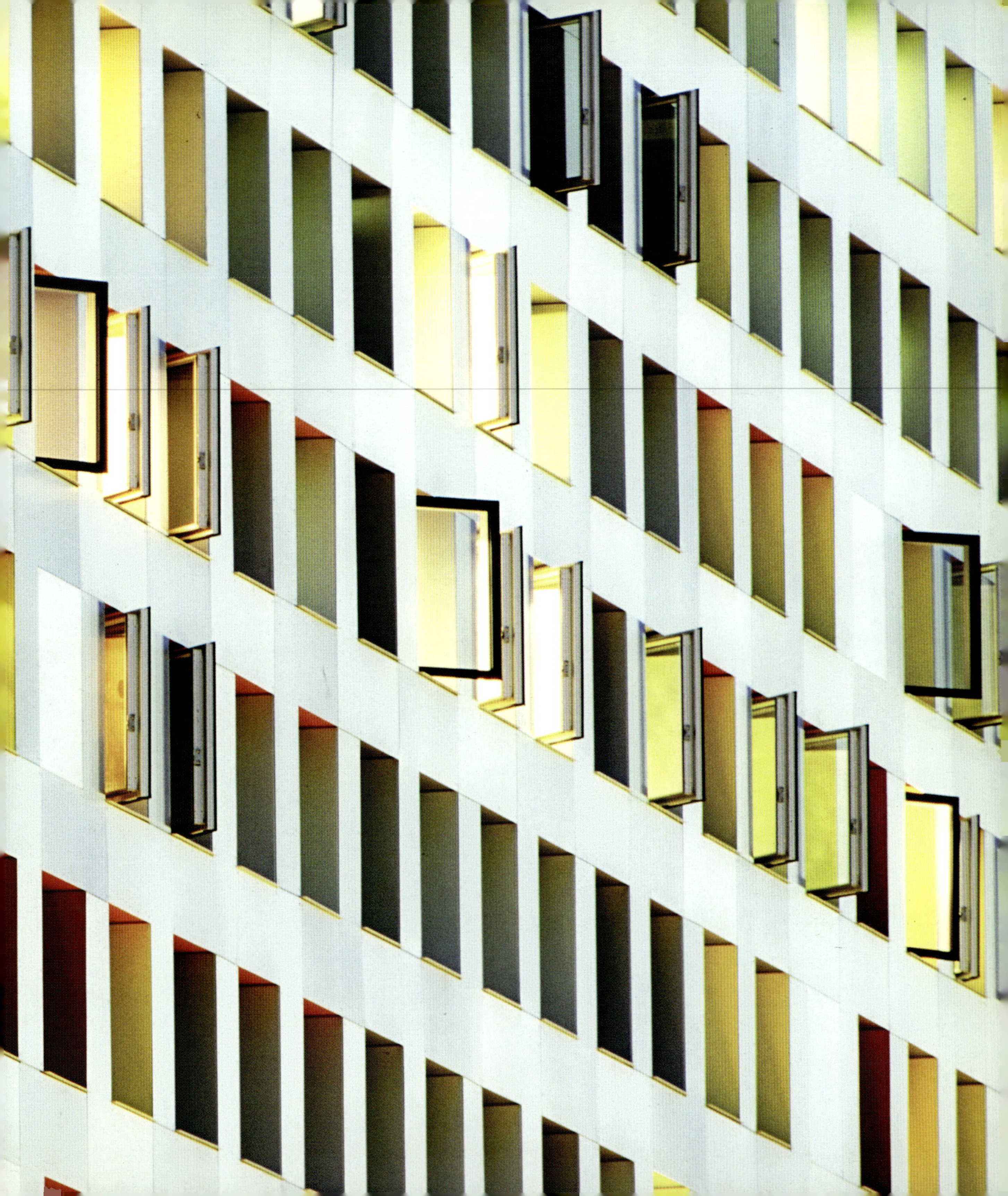

128 COMPLETED CONSTRUCTION

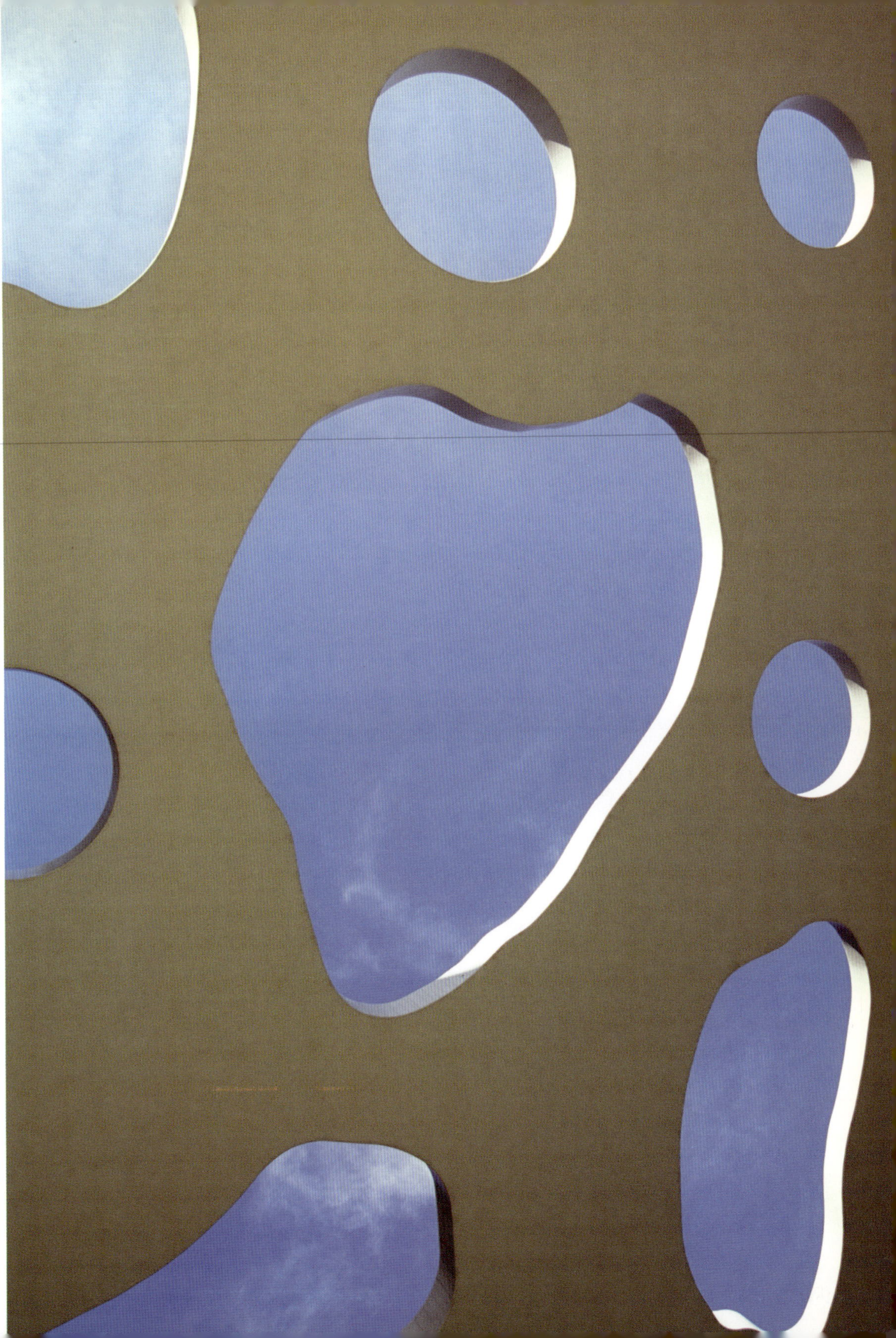

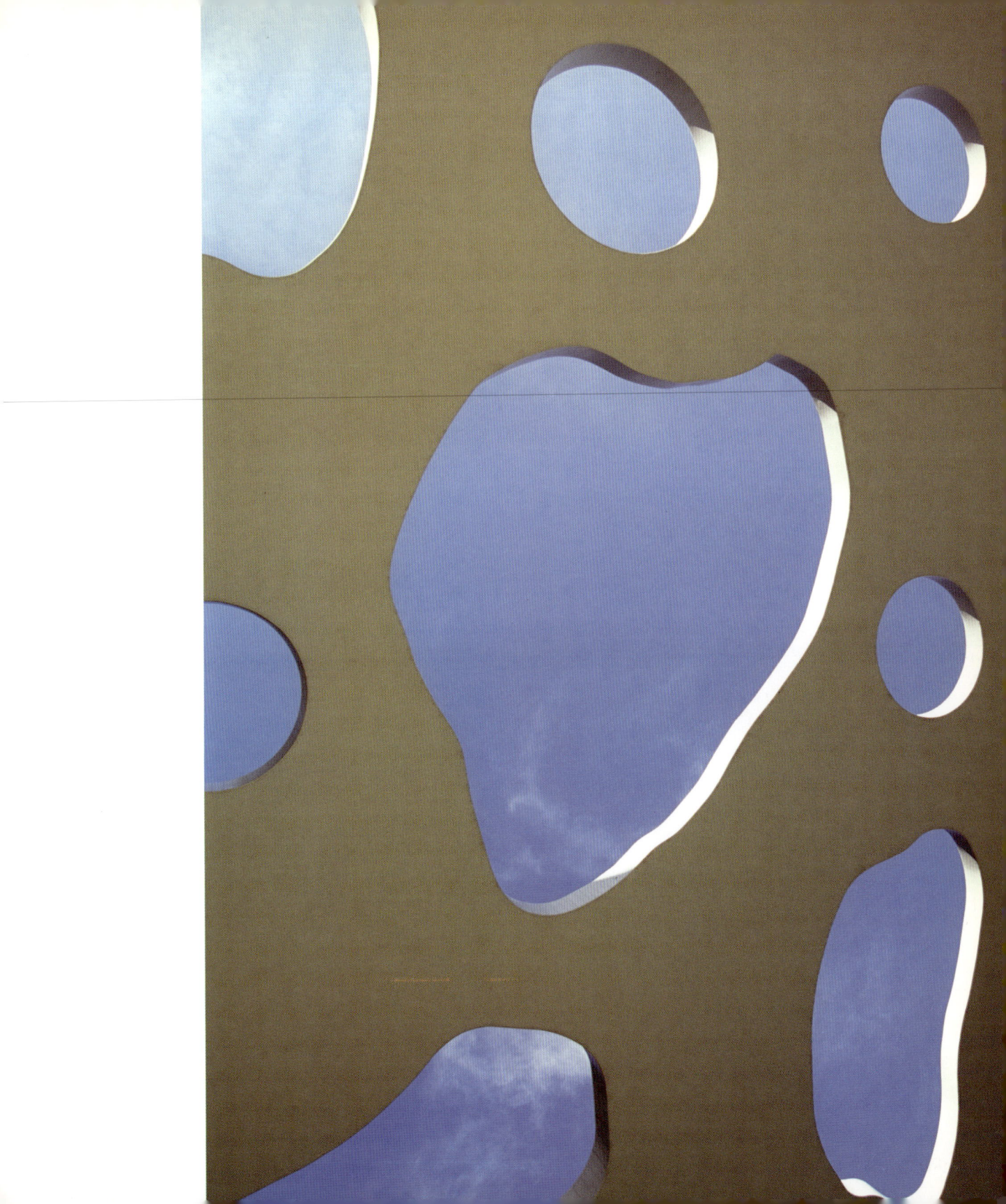

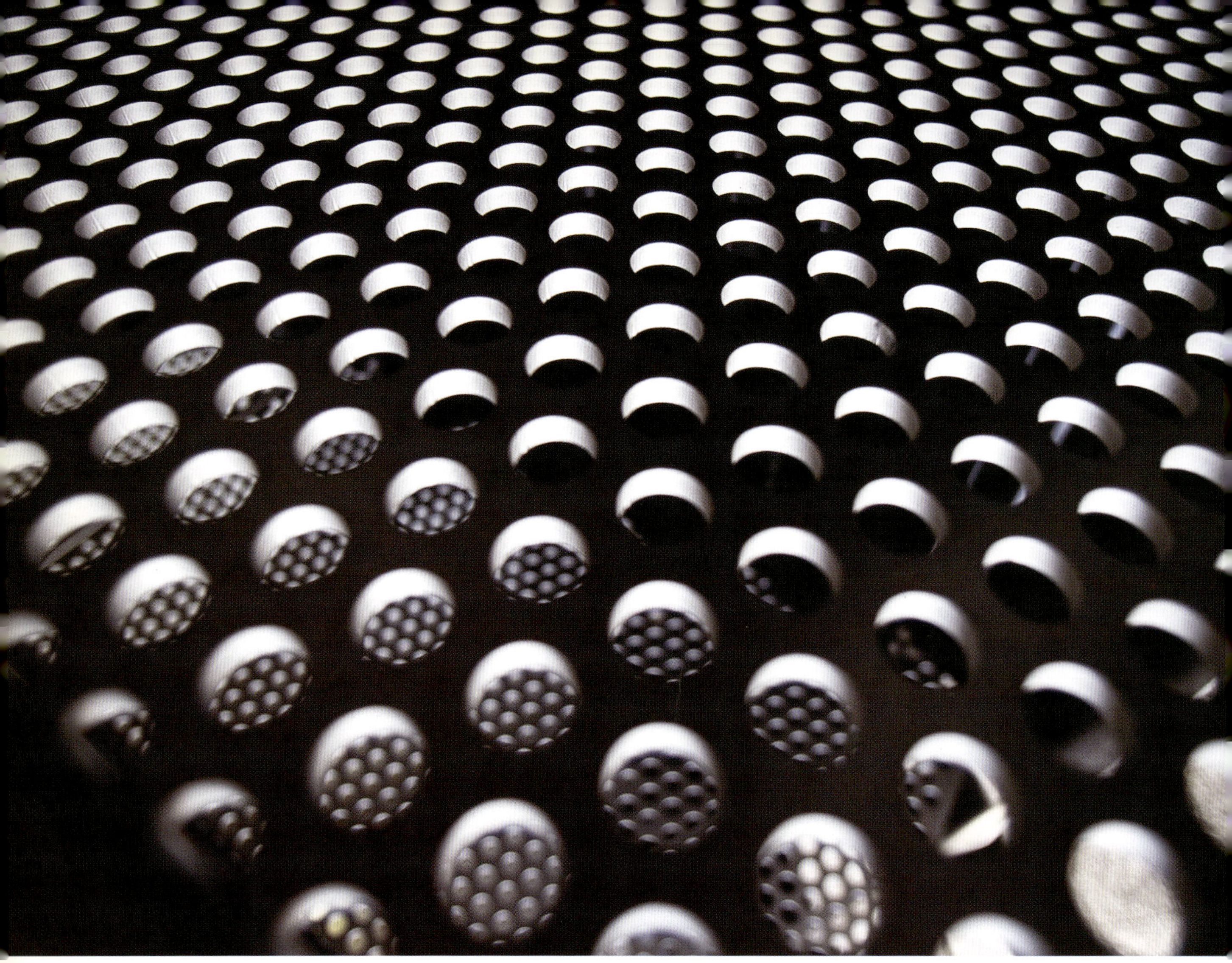

COMPLETED CONSTRUCTION   131

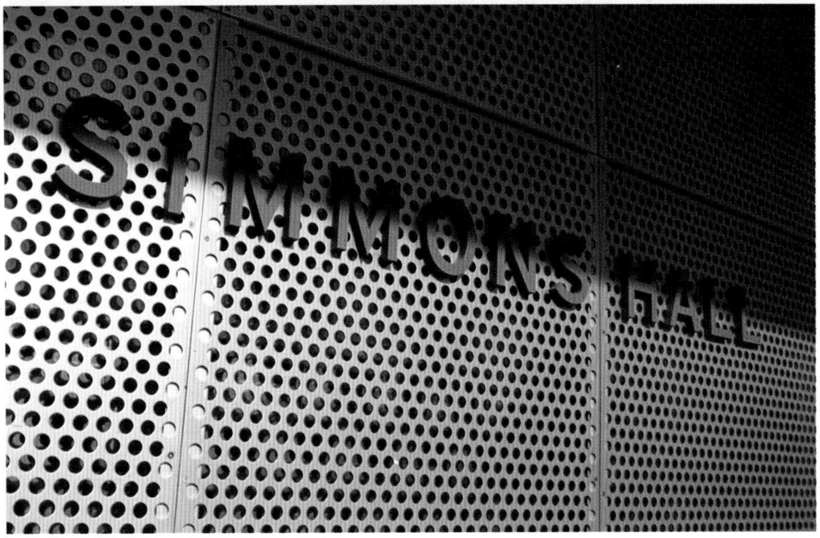
SIMMONS HALL

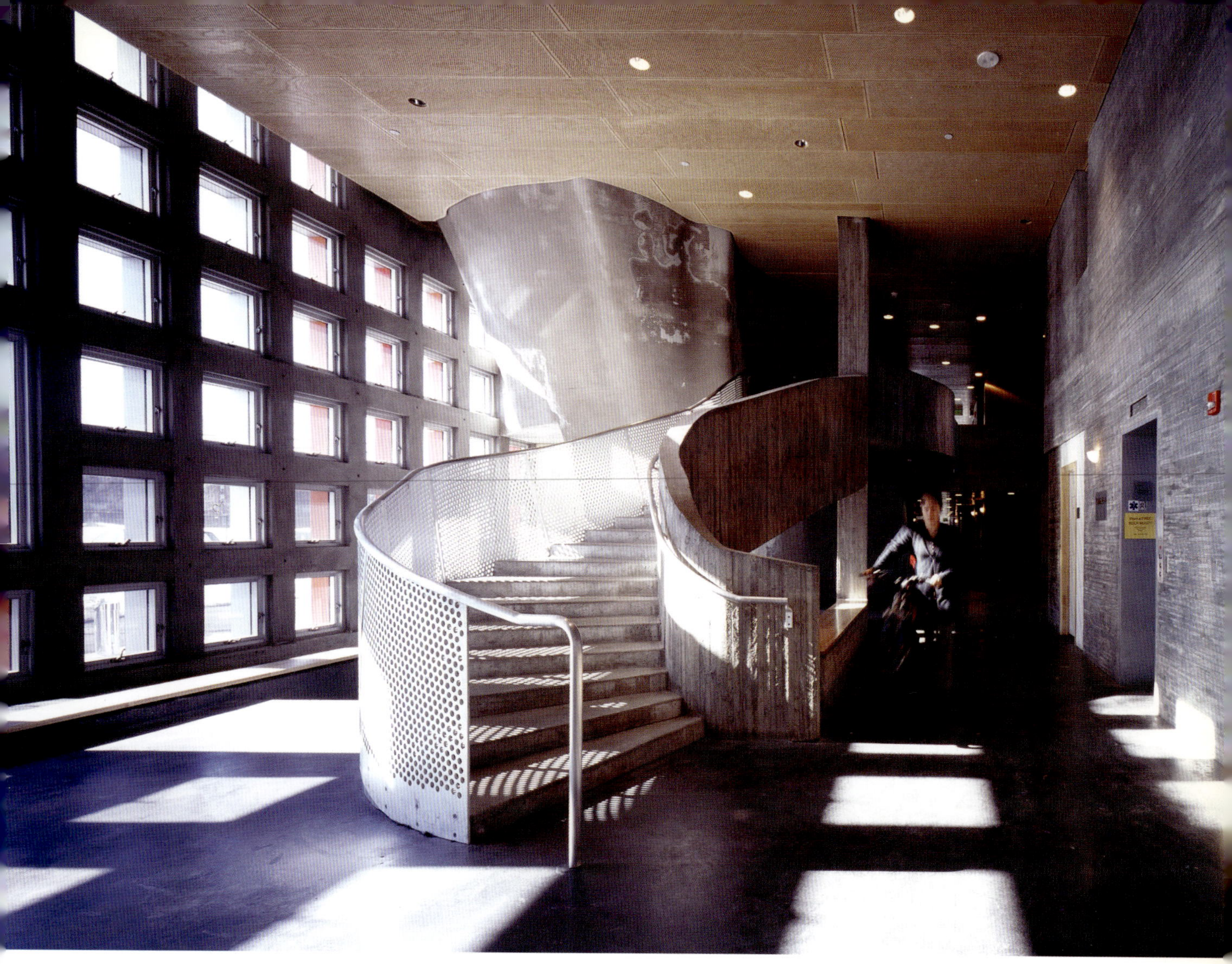

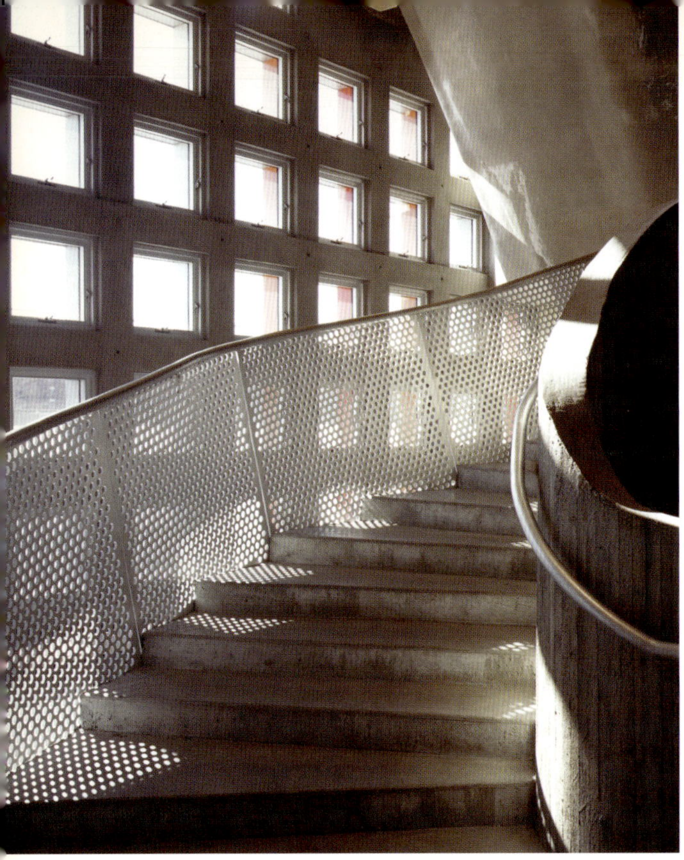

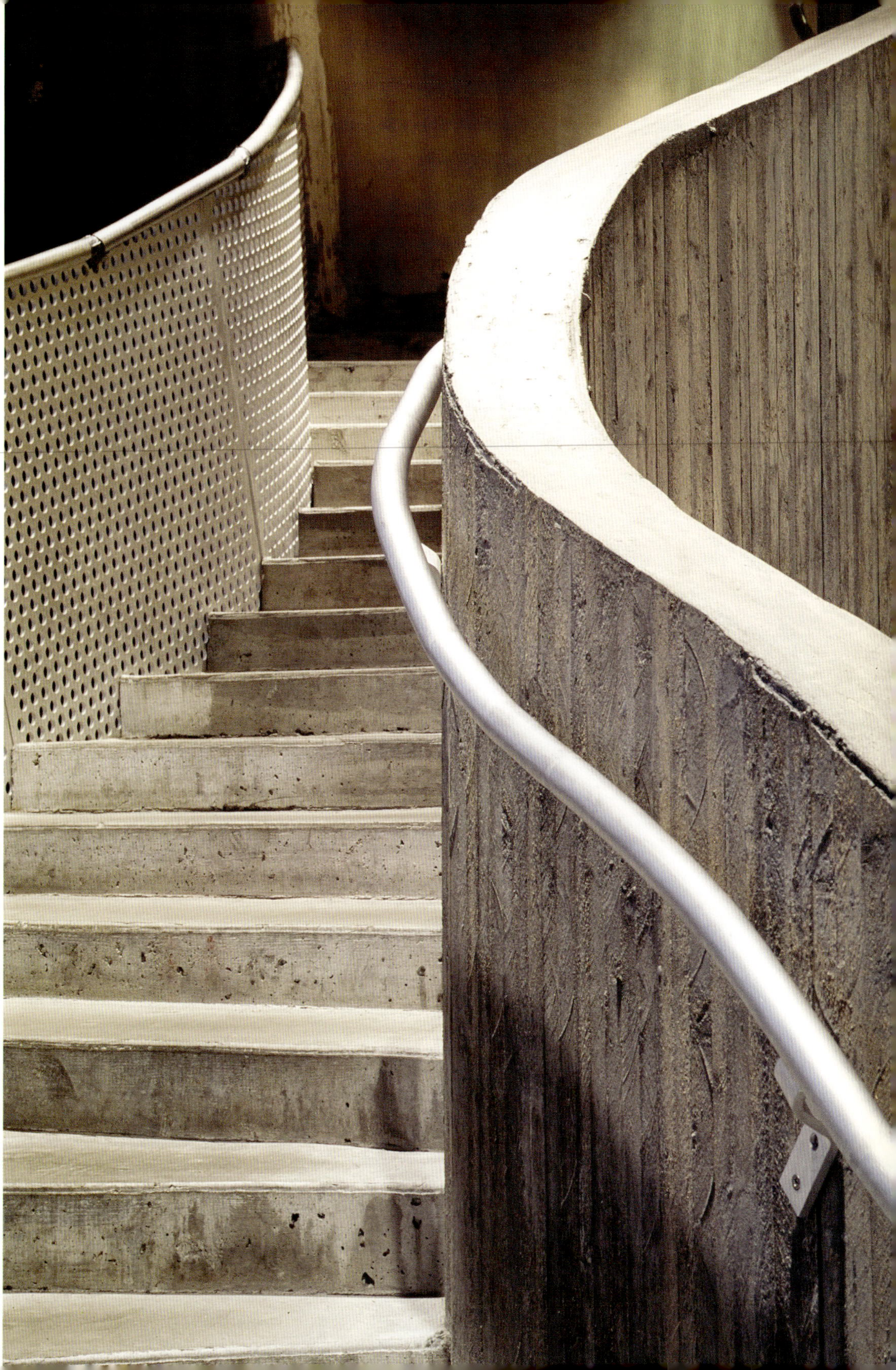

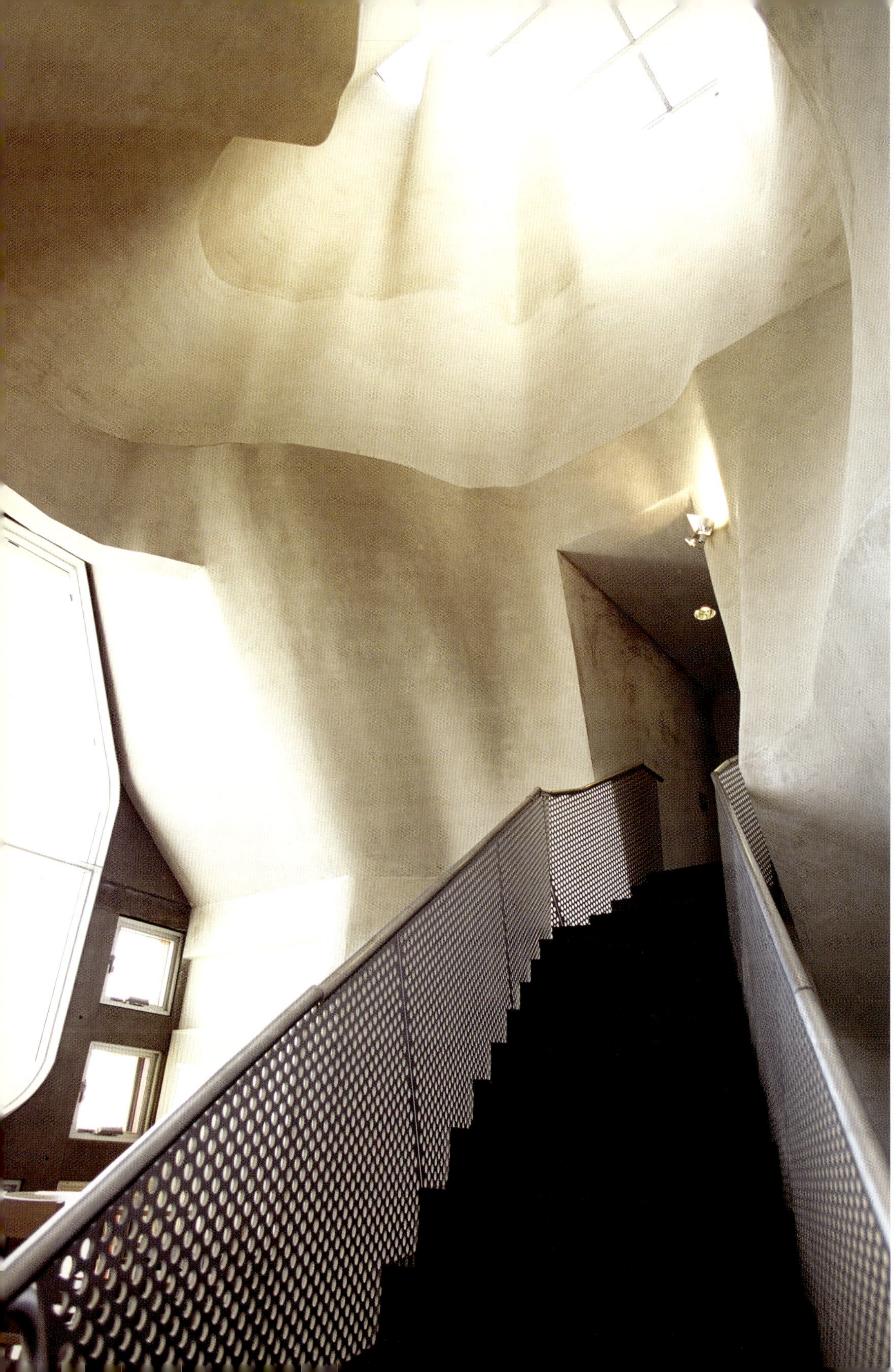

COMPLETED CONSTRUCTION 137

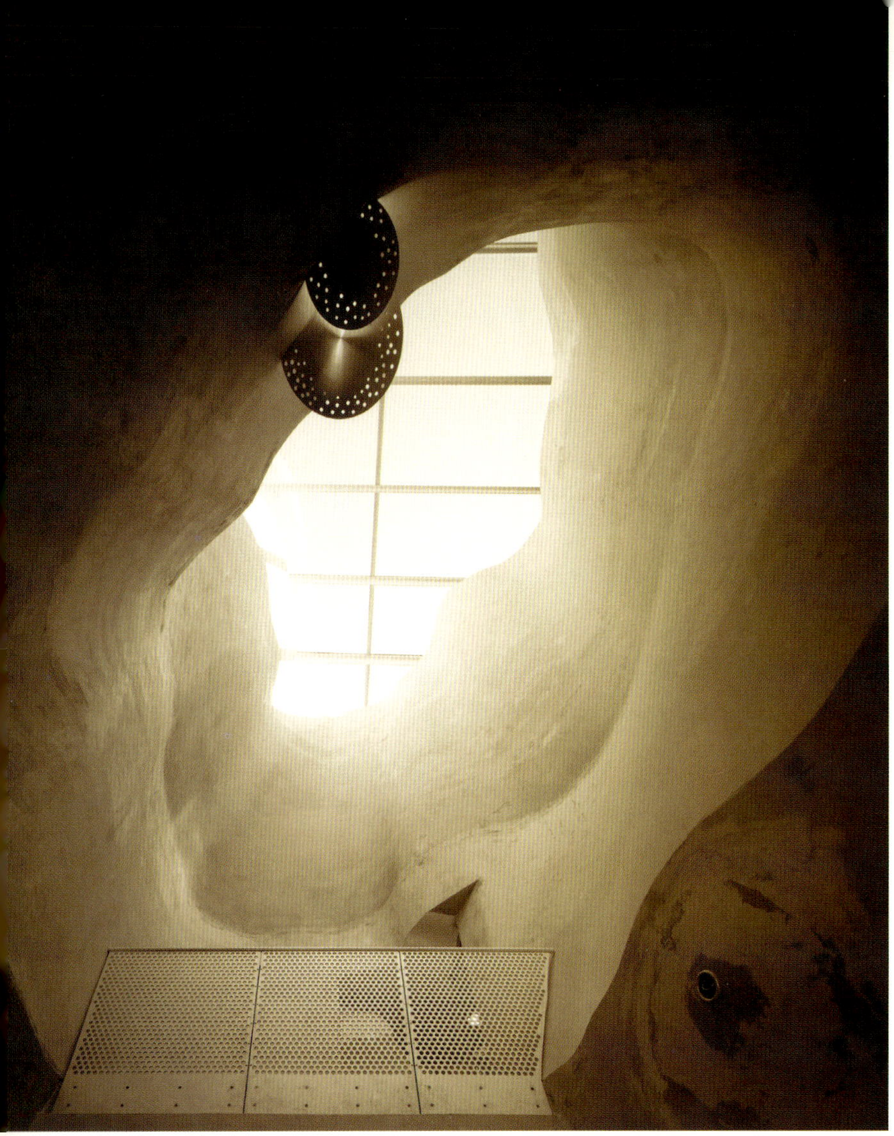

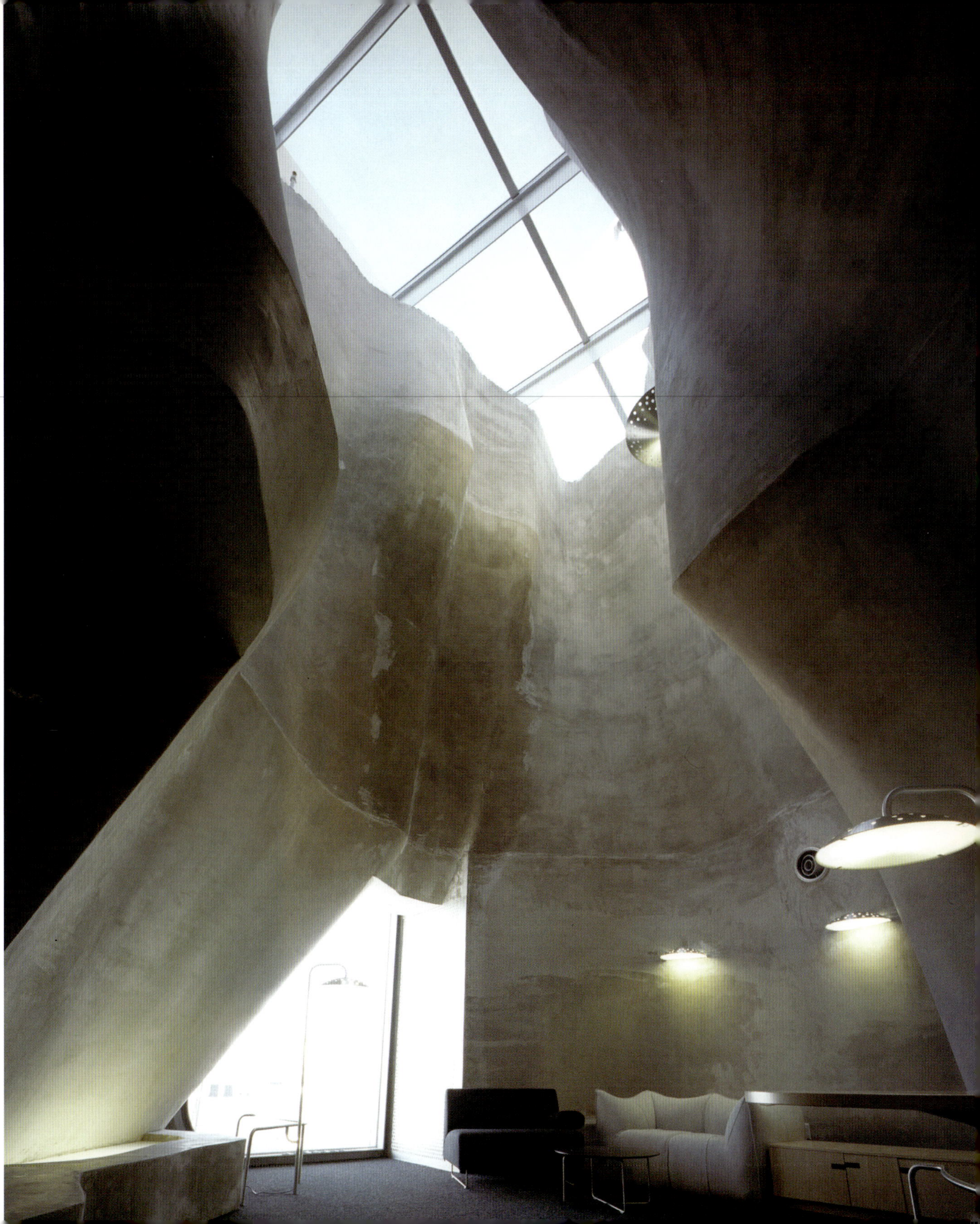

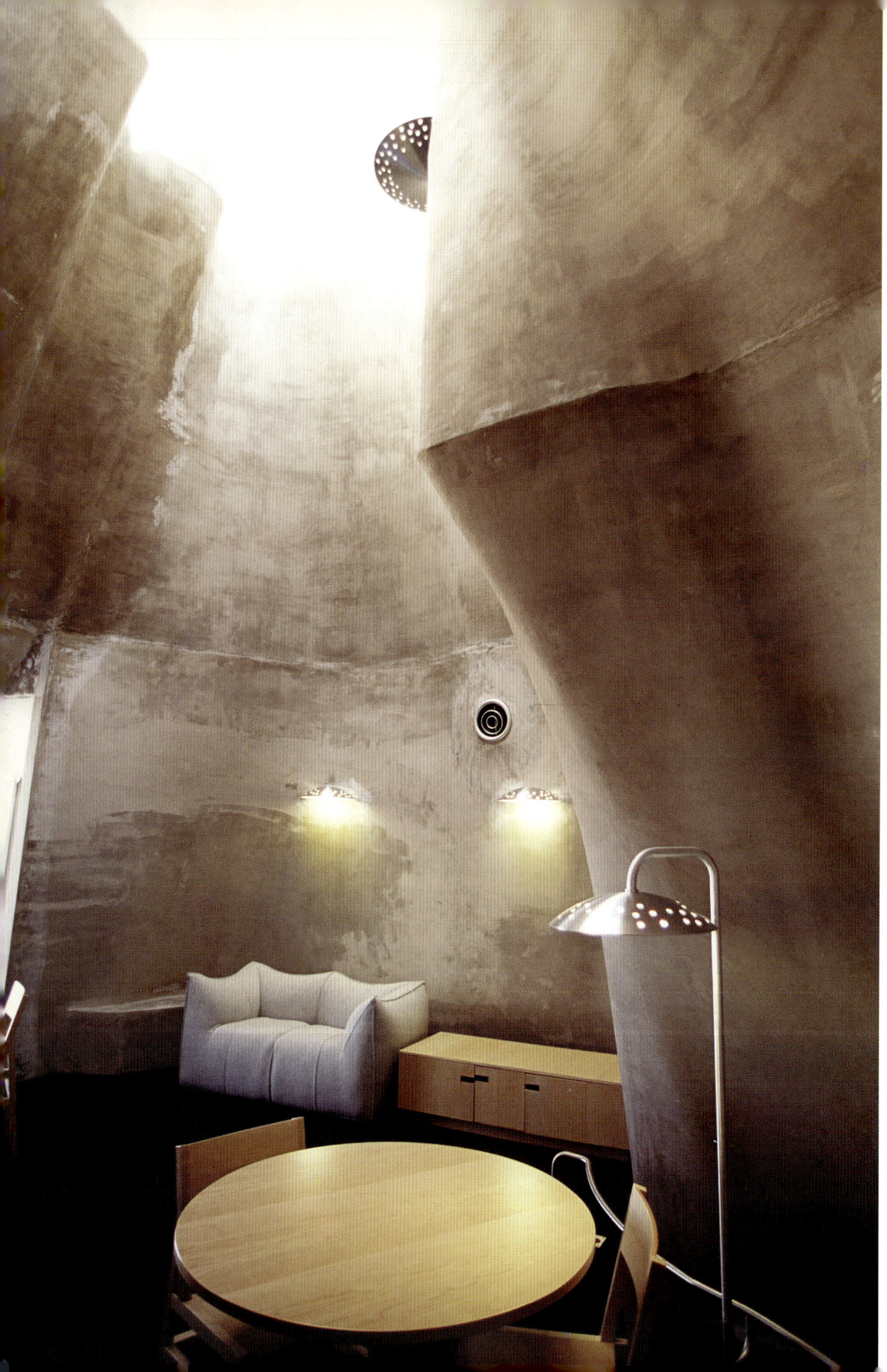

COMPLETED CONSTRUCTION 141

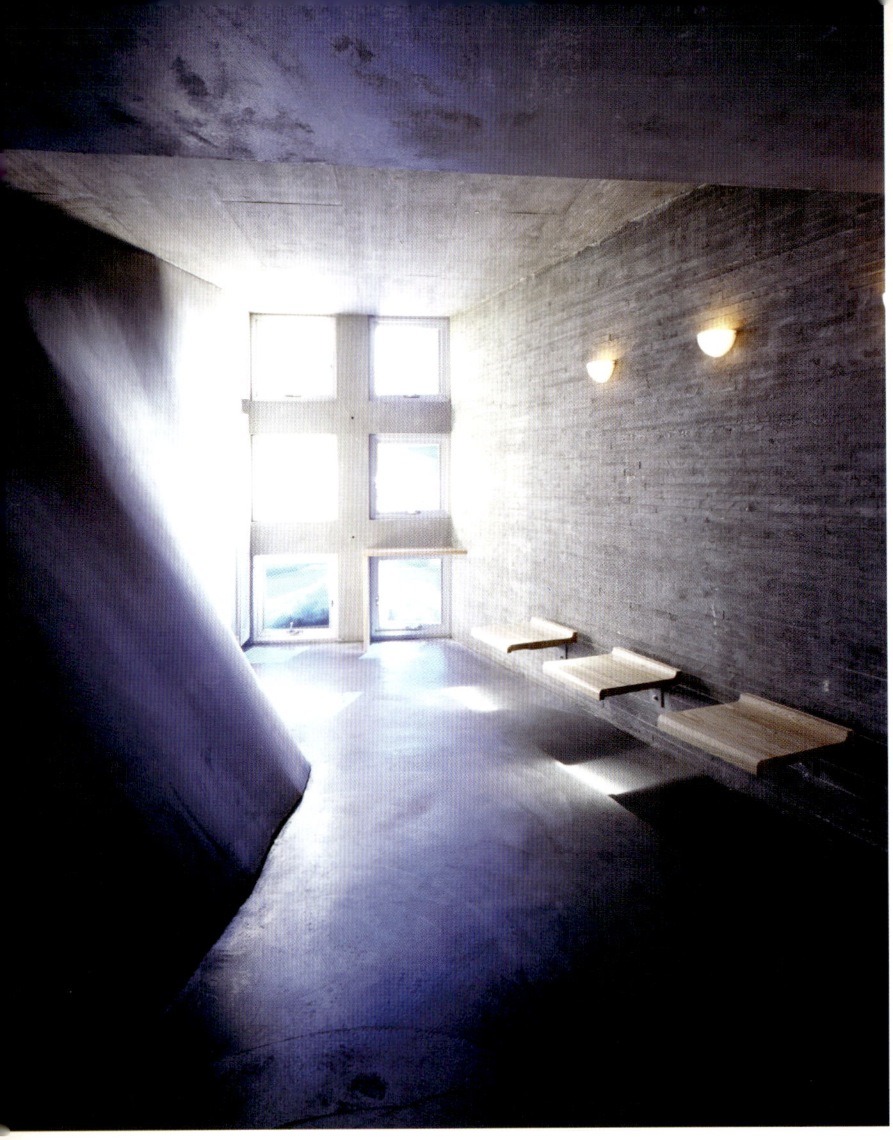

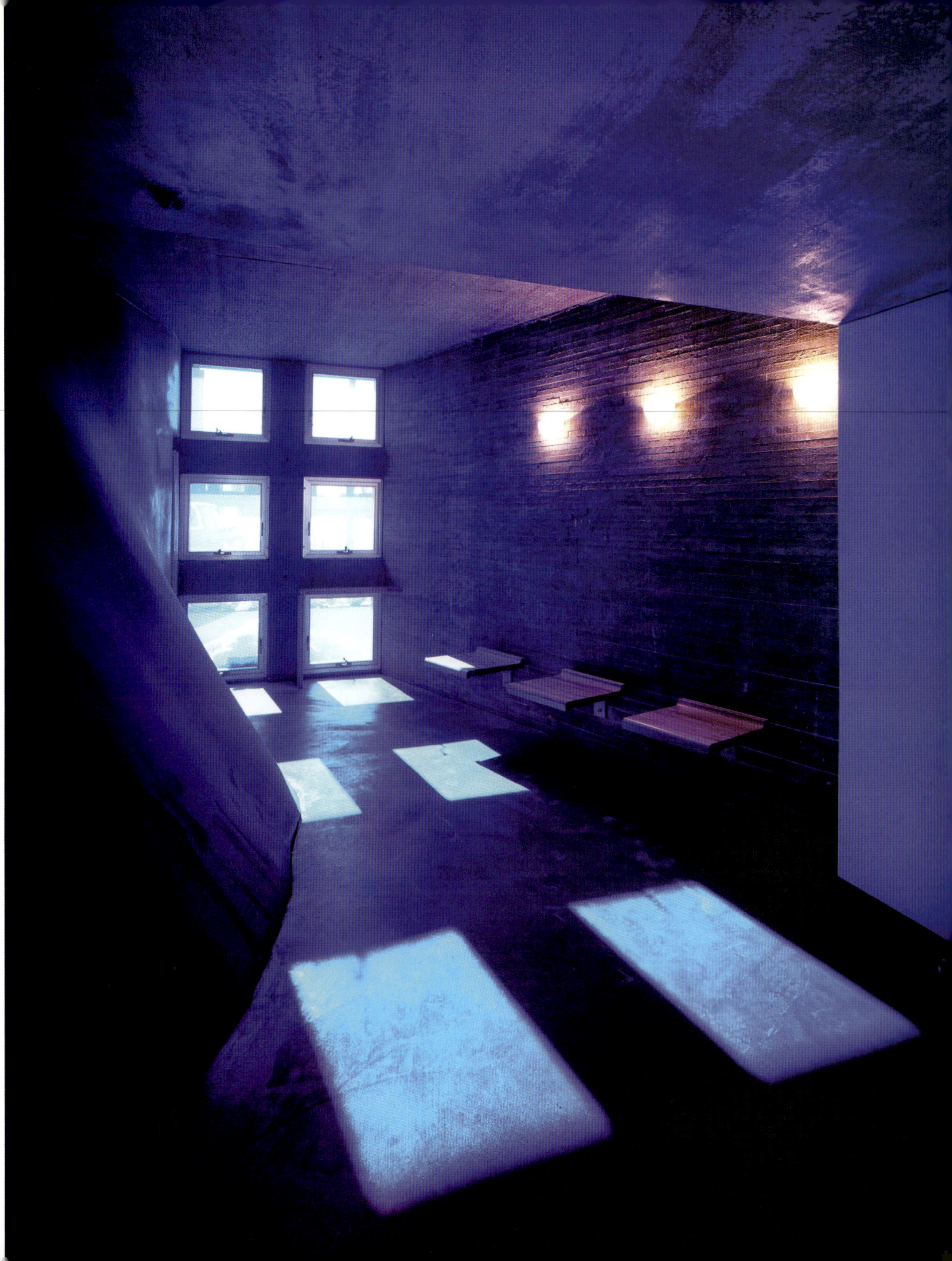

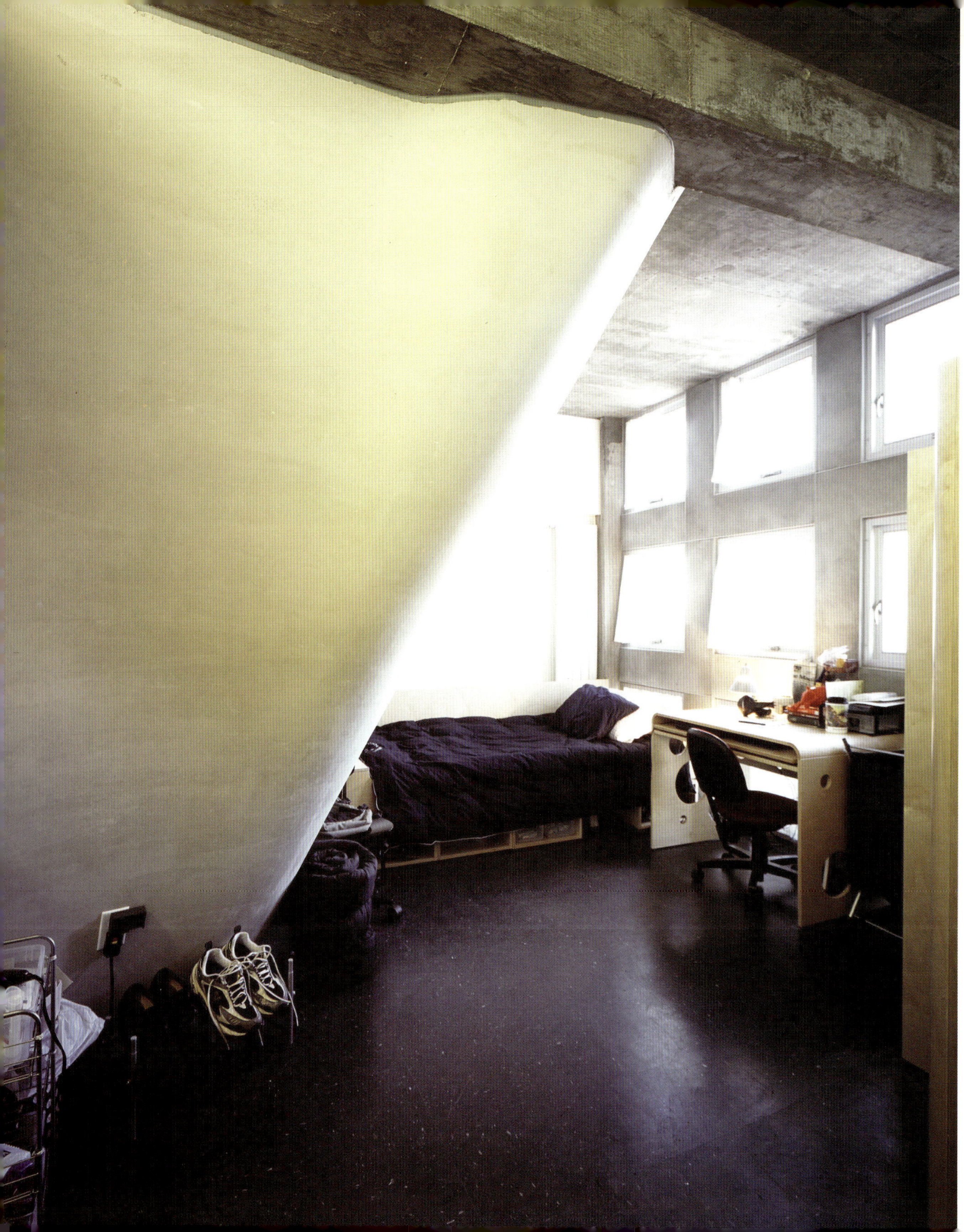

COMPLETED CONSTRUCTION 145

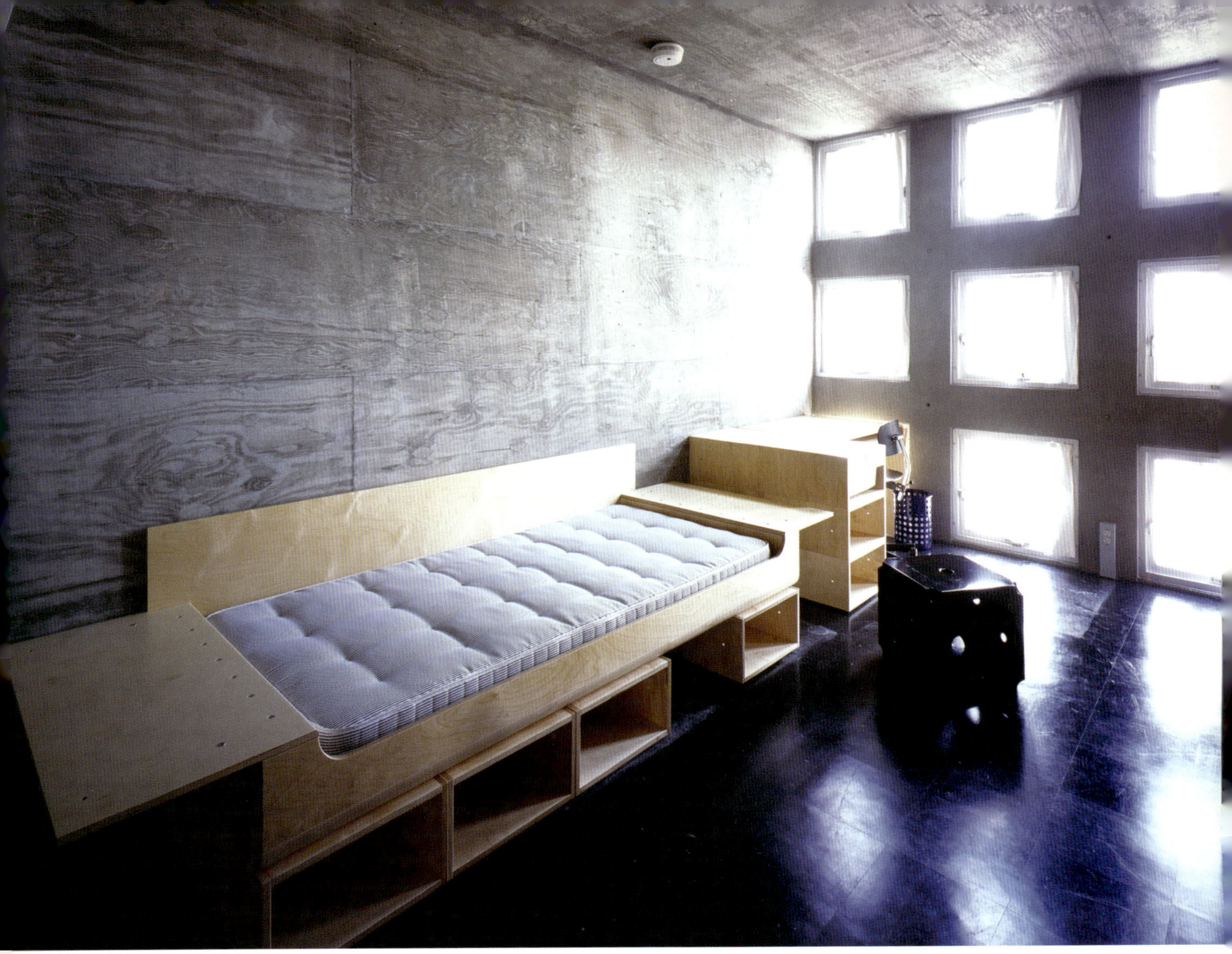

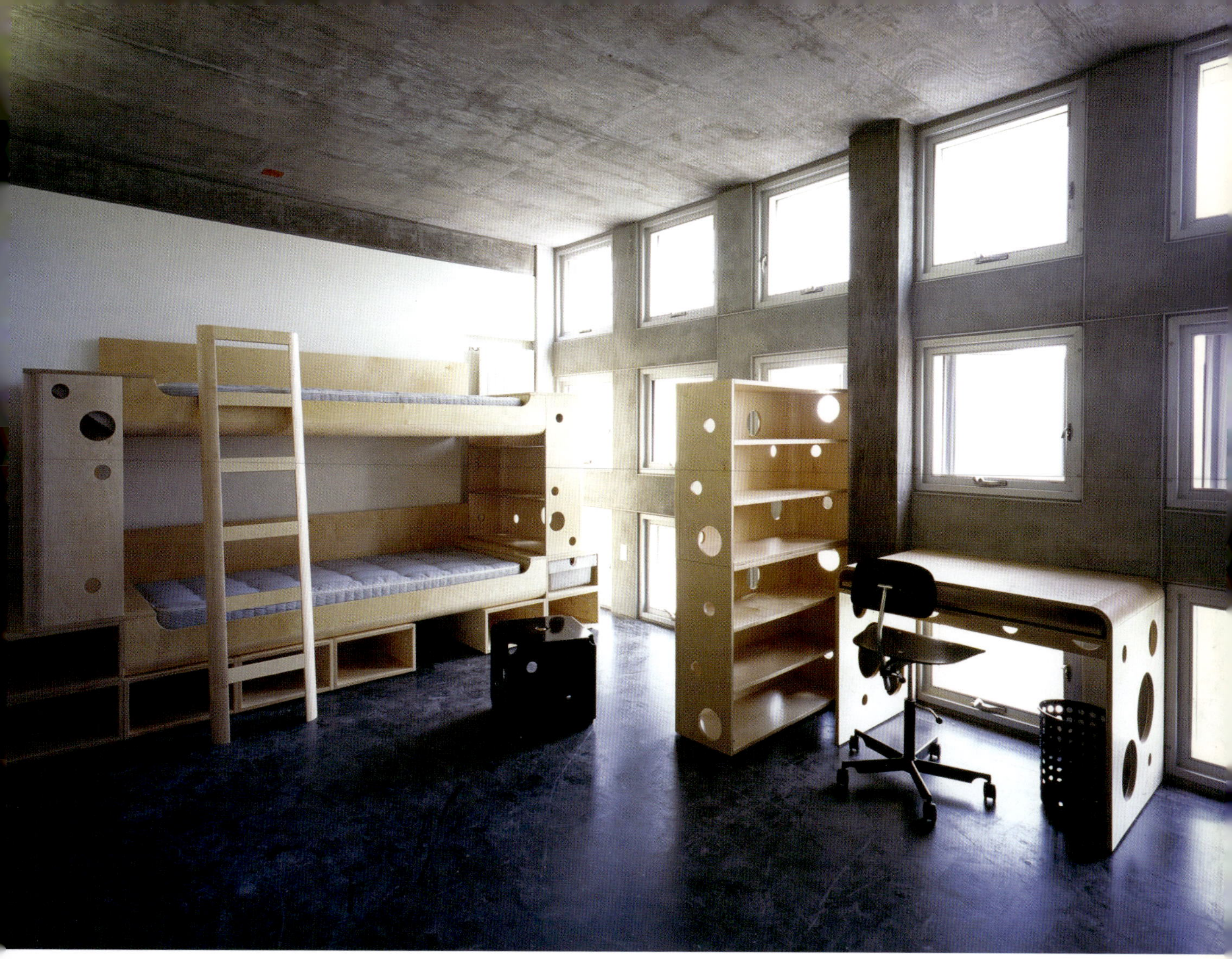

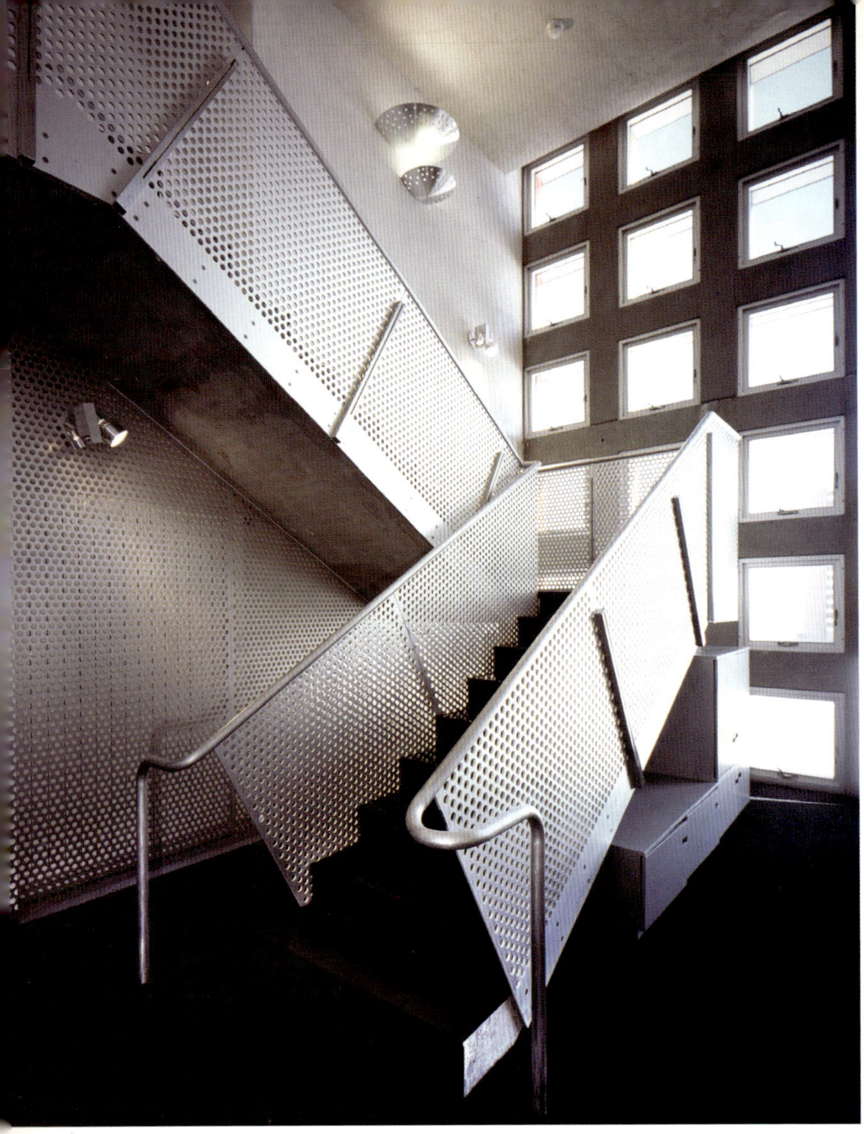

COMPLETED CONSTRUCTION 149

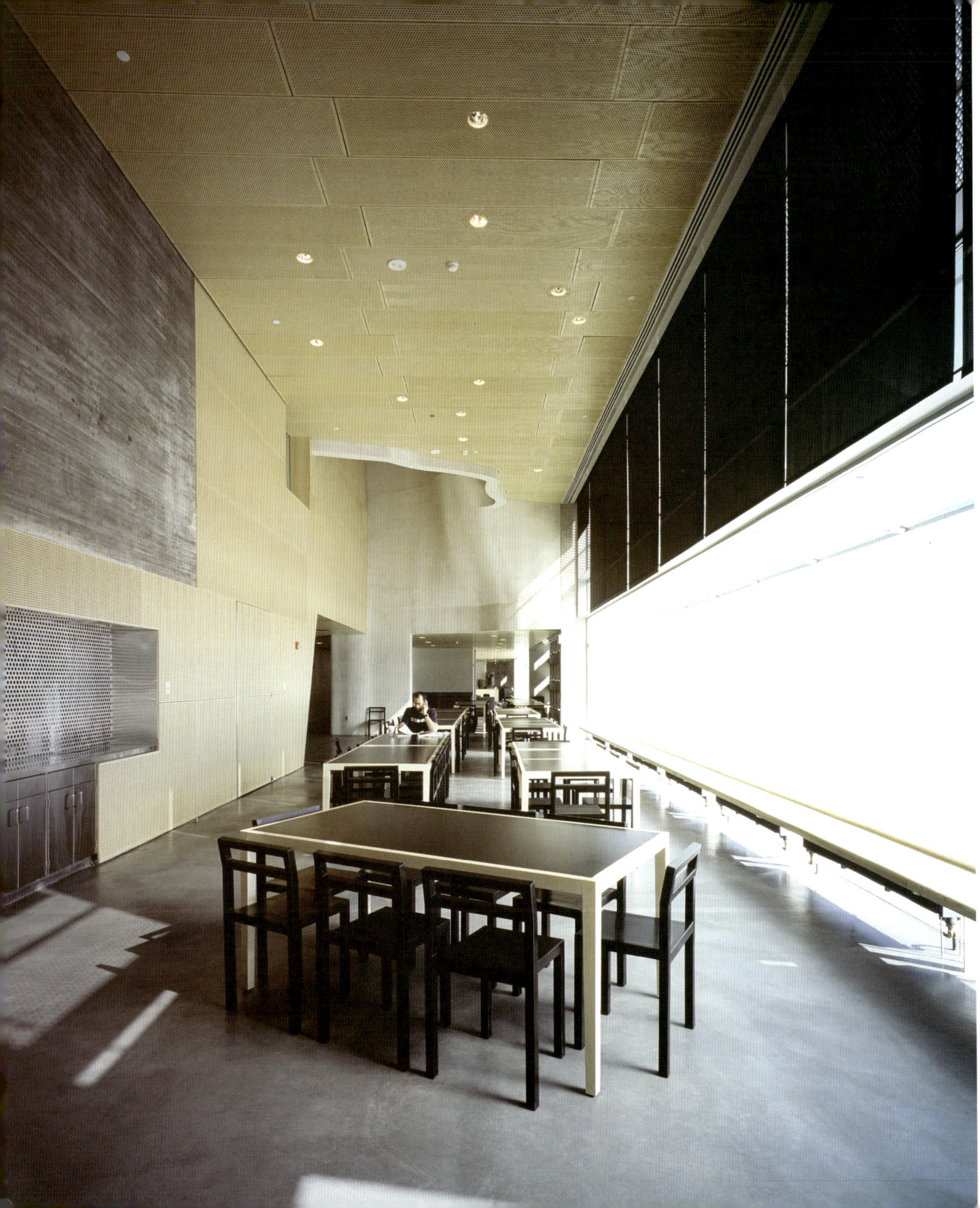

COMPLETED CONSTRUCTION 151

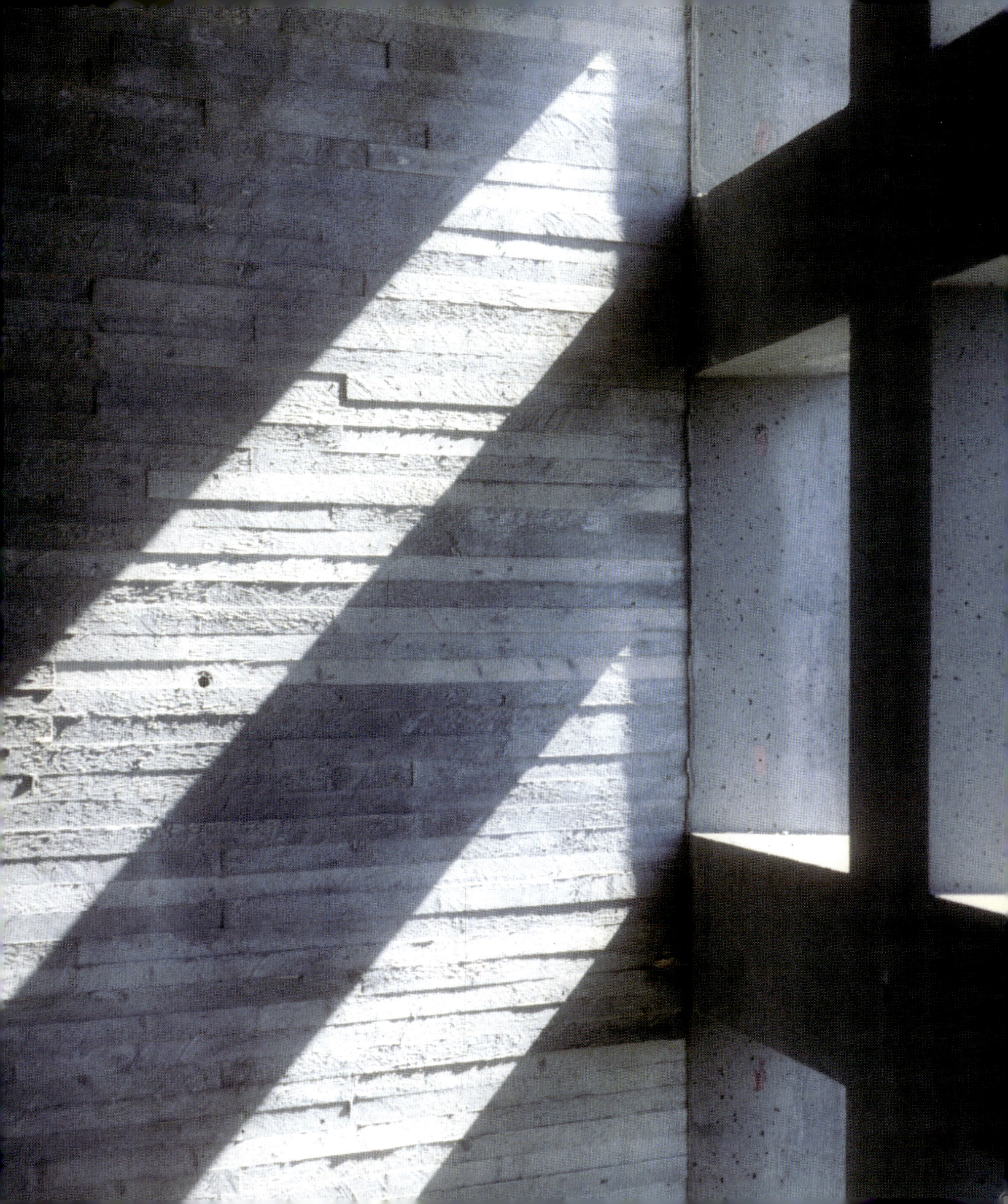

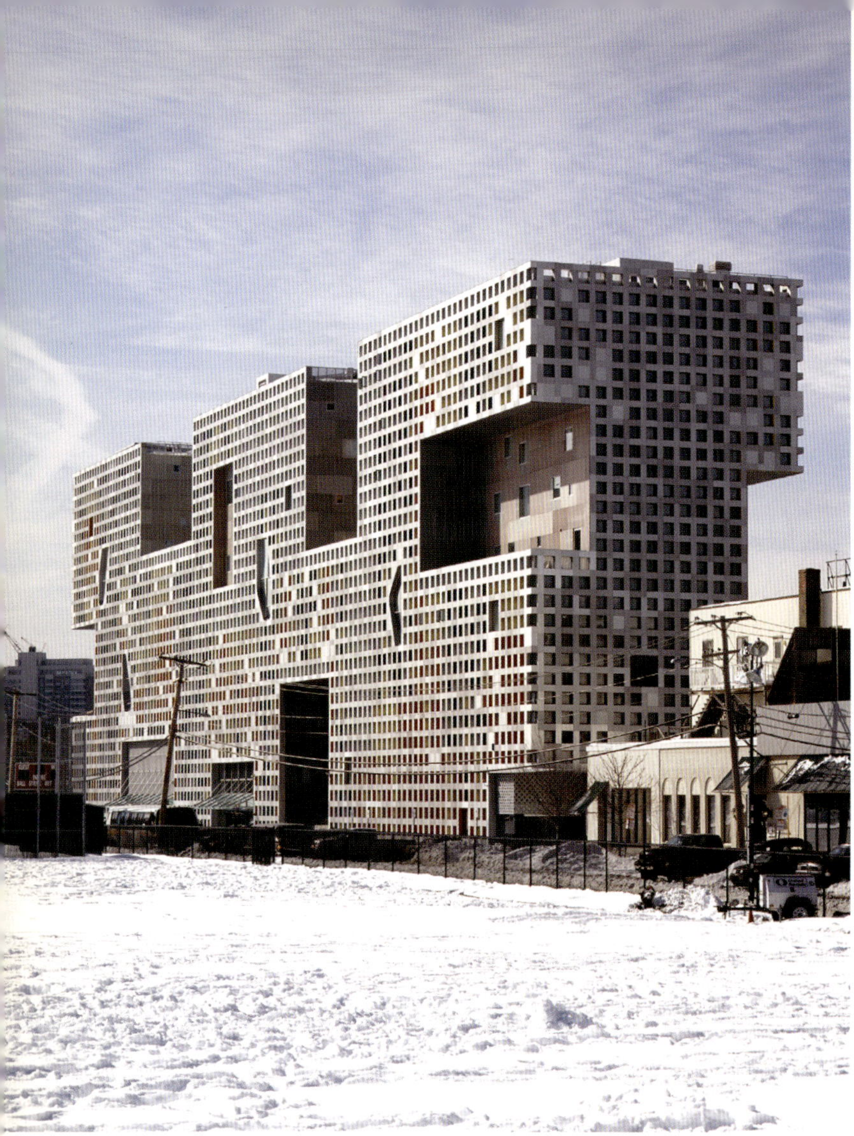

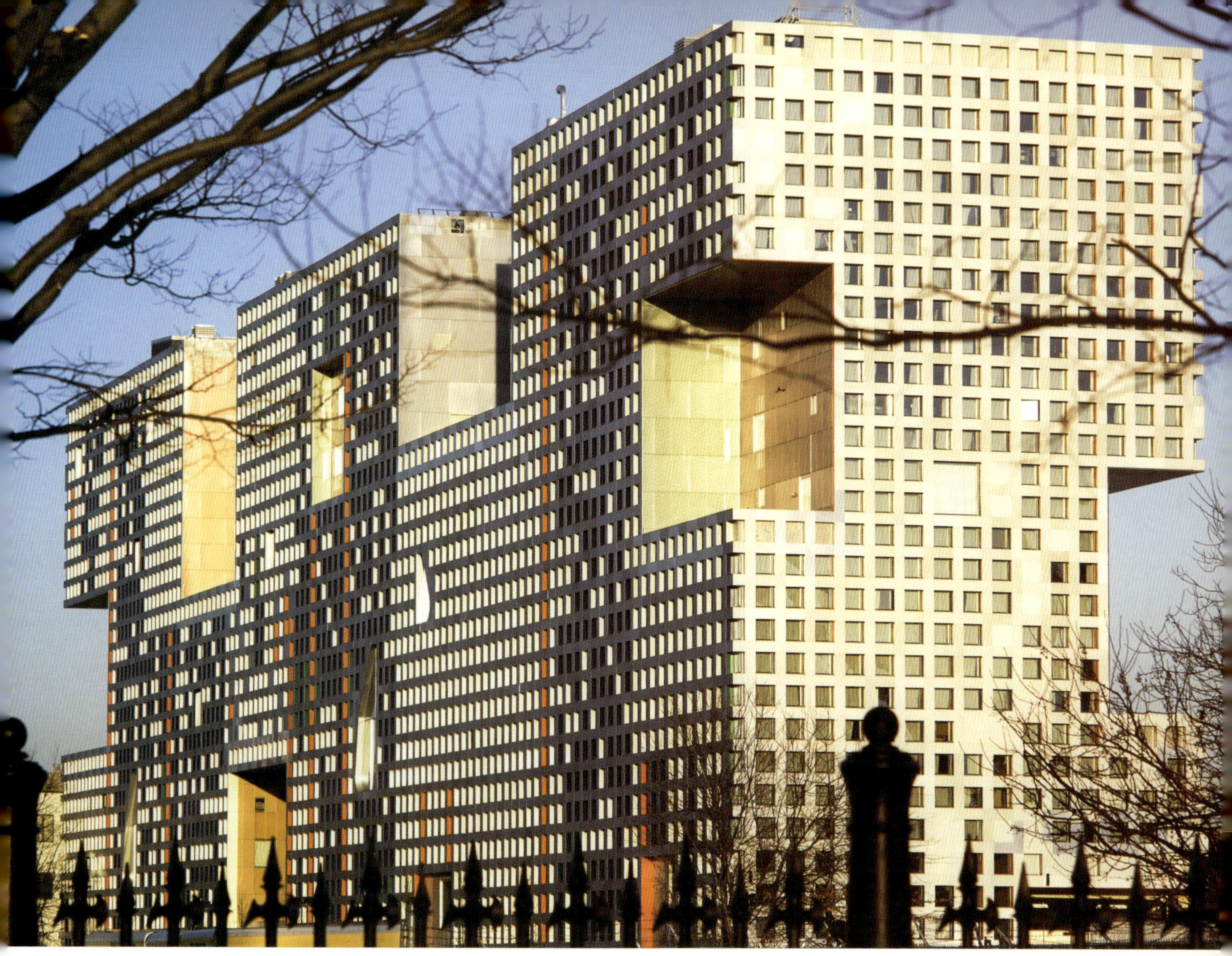

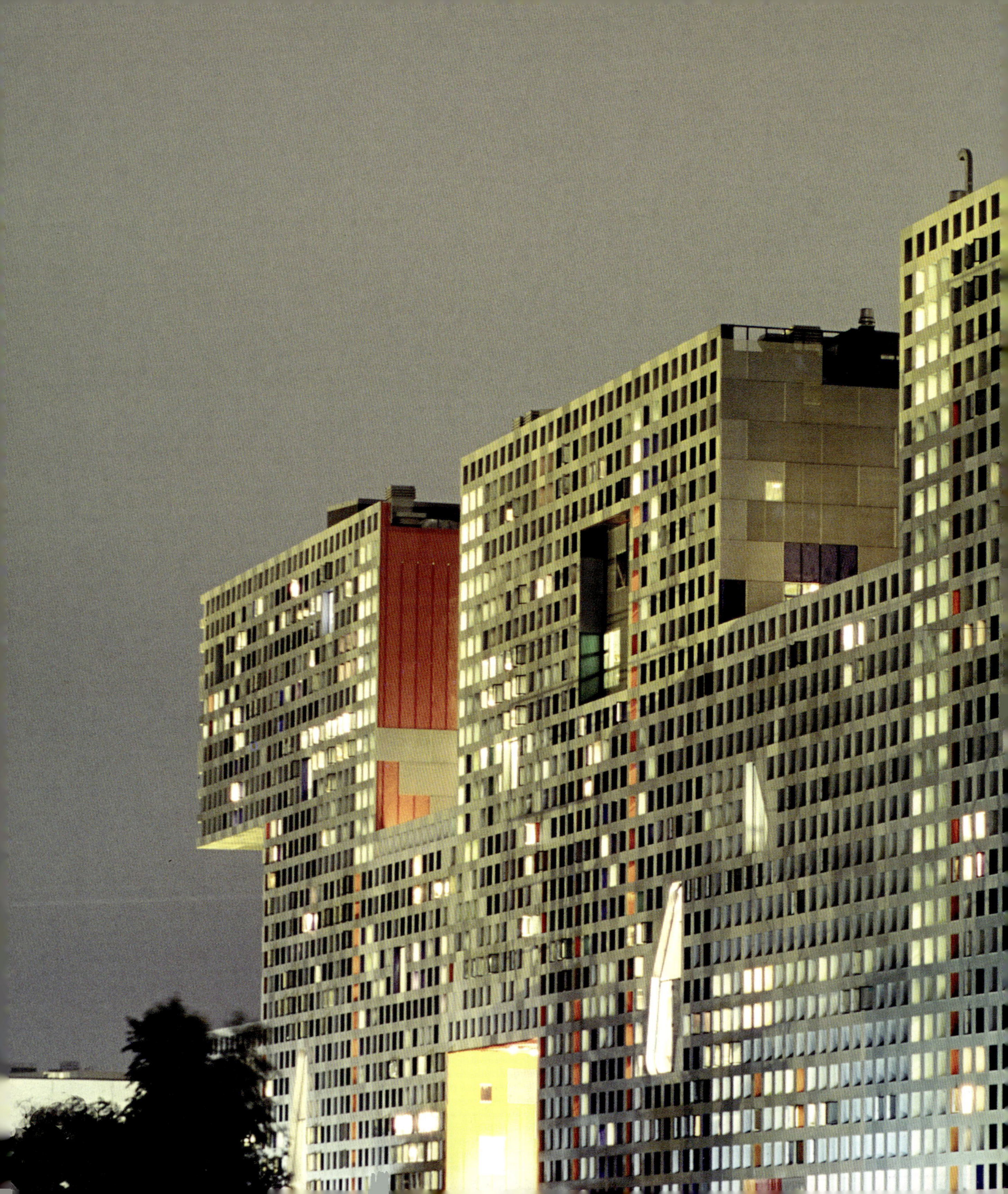

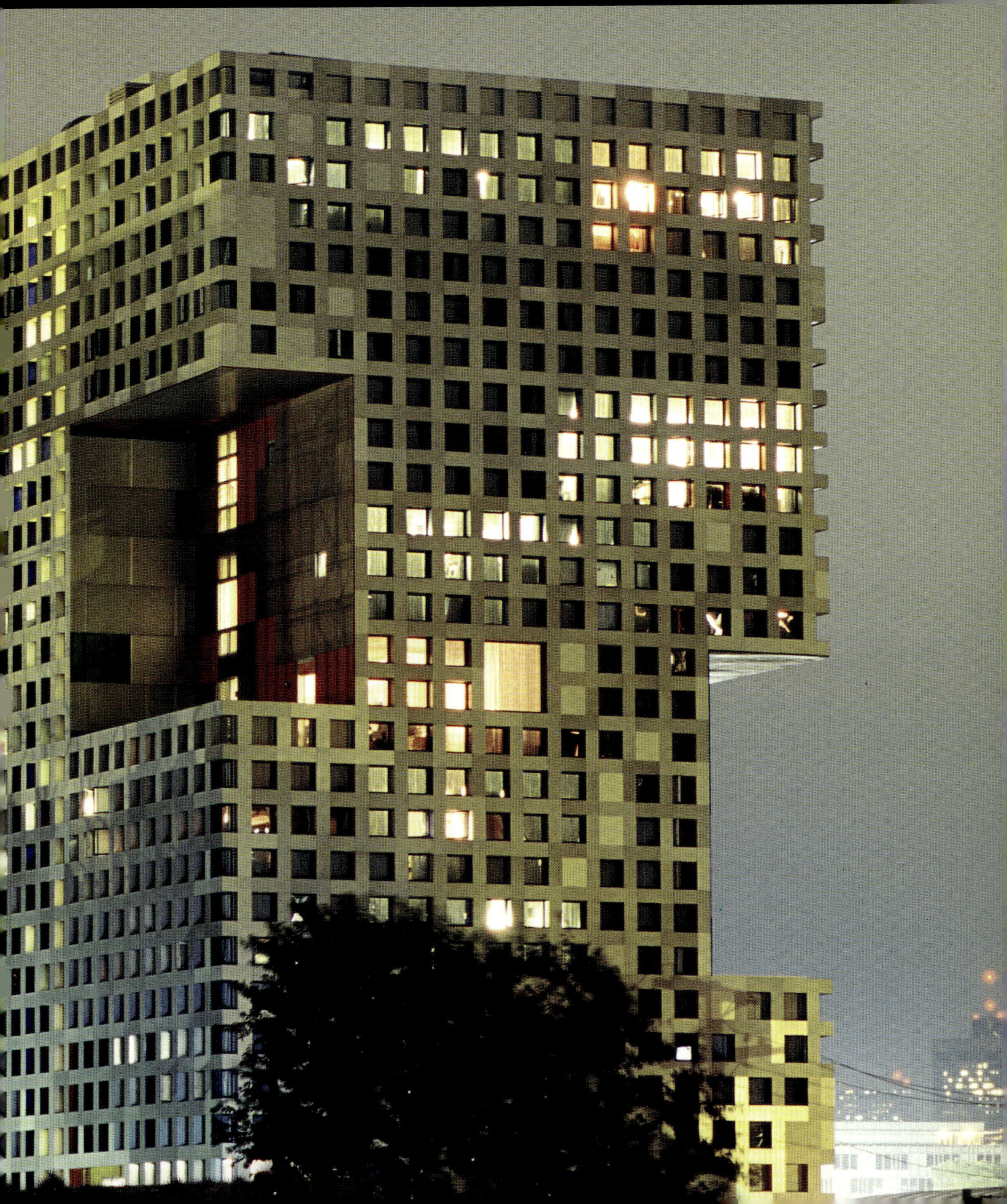

SIMMONS HALL
Yehuda Safran

This essay previously appeared, in a slightly different form, in Domus 85, 8 April 2003

Colin Rowe, the English formalist critic who spent most of his academic career in America, regards MIT's campus in Boston as having set a disastrous precedent for the urban design of the university campus. With Alvar Aalto's dorms and Eero Saarinen's Kresge Auditorium and Chapel, the institution created the paradigm of the building as object. As a result, every campus from coast to coast was transformed into an exhibition of unrelated works by ostensibly prominent architects in a way that could not have happened before 1950.

Half a century later, we have a fair chance to see another model of urban density emerging from the same university campus. If Le Corbusier offered prototypical forms of housing for the communities of workers and Dominican monks at the Unité and La Tourette, respectively, MIT's Simmons Hall is Steven Holl's attempt to do the same for the student community.

In Holl's hands, the dormitory is no longer simply a place to sleep. Offering a full-fledged social program, it becomes a social condenser in the true sense of the term. Holl has provided for a wide range of social activities including communal eating and restaurant facilities that connect directly with the street and a series of common rooms that burrow through the different layers of the building. There is a 125-seat theater and associated sports areas arranged outside in tandem with Dan Graham's art installation, *Yin and Yang*, which in a way mirrors the building.

If student life is a rehearsal for future life in civil society, this project can be said to revolutionize everyday life in the university, releasing the ordinary street into a world of experiment and play as an alternative to the dangers of political apathy and personal isolation—the negative extremes of the student experience. In so doing, it decisively alters our way of seeing the public life of the street and the organization of living space. Diagonally opposite Aalto's Baker House, where the floor plane undulates horizontally, Holl introduces dramatic shifts in height, which augment the level of interaction between private spaces and the larger collective gathering spaces. An increase in the amount of collective interior space is matched by a new measure conferred on the individual dwelling units. Consequently, the two confront each other as markers of public and private places.

One hundred forty meters long and ten stories tall, Simmons Hall is a slice of urban space that echoes Holl's own earlier preoccupation with the edge of the city. Relatively wide corridors connecting the rooms turn the hallway into a streetlike environment that benefits from the porous morphology by providing unexpected openings, lounges, and common halls. Unlike the orthogonal matrix of individual units, the public condensers consist of undulating surfaces with unforeseen sources of light from above that bring daylight into the heart of the structure. These collective spaces are intended to bring students together, to provoke interaction and dialogue.

This raw, minimally clad building, marked by an ingenuity that is evident not only in tectonic terms but also in the use of color and a deliberately rough surface articulation, seems to offer just such an environment of community. It is perhaps the first time that a brutalist language has been attempted on this scale in a major university in the United States since Paul Rudolph's once controversial, now paradigmatic, Yale Art and Architecture Building.

Terms such as porous, permeable, screen, net, porosity, pore, aperture, passageway, sieve, honeycomb, riddle, sponge, opening, and hole are among the words and concepts elaborated in the early stages of the urban design competition that Holl won to build the project four years ago. Four large dorms were originally conceived and projected as a street-oriented urban order for the area—all featured the same degree of porousness. This overall plan, of which only one dormitory has been realized, refers to the predetermined lexical field, with its "multiple roots," that shatter the linear unity of language itself; it transforms Holl's conceptual sphere into a rhizome. For him, the crucial question is knowledge of things, seen as the convergence of infinite relationships: past and future, real and possible. His building ceaselessly establishes connections between semiotic chains, the organization of power, space, and circumstances relative to the arts, sciences, and social differentiation.

In relation to diverse acts—perceptive, mimetic, gestural and cognitive—it forms a bulb with its many layers inside out. The unit implies multiplicities of varieties of measurement. Multiplicity increases the number of possible connections. The plane of consistency is the grid—it is external to all of these connections and at the same time makes them possible. Individual rooms, groups, social formations, accelerations, and transformations are always in direct communication with the exterior. Large open spaces with light chimneys are opposed in every way to traditional dorms with their endless corridors. The separation of structures or the cutting of a single structure signifies rupture. As a rhizome it may be broken, shattered at a given spot, but it will start up again on one of its old lines, or a new line. In this sense Holl's work asks that everything should be precisely named, described, and located in space and time. Its multiplicity conjugates its heterogeneous reality. The student community is being offered not a machine for living, but a city segment to experiment with and to discover.

Holl exploits the potential of a raw skin stretched on a rigid grid of small windows, nine to a room. Because he made three rows of windows with three windows each, a module of a prefabricated panel, he achieved loftier ceilings than those specified by the university's standards. Working with the innovative engineer Guy Nordenson, Holl devised the Perfcon structure that fuses window, wall, and structure in prefabricated pieces. This unique process establishes the rhythm of internal and external wall surfaces—a distinctive aspect of the design.

Henry David Thoreau once said, "How could youth better learn to live than by at once trying to experiment with living?" believing that students should not play at life or study it while the community supports them at this expensive game, but rather earnestly live it from the beginning to the end of their academic years. Thoreau might have preferred the students to have built the dormitory with their own hands, but Holl's Simmons Hall allows its residents to realize Thoreau's ideal.

CREDITS

CLIENT
Massachusetts Institute of Technology, Cambridge, MA
Senior Project Manager
Jonathan Himmel
Project Director
Thomas Murray, Casali Group, Inc., Somerville, MA

DESIGN ARCHITECT
Steven Holl Architects, New York
Design Architects
Steven Holl, Timothy Bade
Project Architect
Timothy Bade
Assisant Project Architects
Ziad Jameleddine, Anderson Lee
Project Team
Peter Burns, Gabriela Barman-Kramer, Annette Goderbauer, Mimi Hoang, Ziad Jameleddine, Matt Johnson, Erik Langdalen, Anderson Lee, Ron-Hui Lin, Stephen O'Dell, Christian Wassman.

ASSOCIATE ARCHITECT
Perry Dean Rogers/Partners

Partners in Charge
Peter Ringenbach, Charles Rogers
Project Architect
Michael Waters
Project Team
Jeff Fishbien, Samantha Pearson, Brent Stringfellow, Gerry Gutirrez, Brad Prestbo, Alejandro Soto, Mark Wintringer

STRUCTURAL ENGINEER
Guy Nordenson and Associates, New York
Partner
Guy Nordenson
Project Engineer
Christopher Diamond

ENGINEER OF RECORD
Simpson Gumpertz & Heger, Inc.
Partner
James Parker
Project Team
John Thomson, Amy Stern

MEP ENGINEERING
Ove Arup & Partners, New York and Cambridge, MA

Partner
Mahadev Raman
Project Managers
Mark Walsh-Cooke, Nigel Tonks

LIGHTING DESIGN
Fisher Marantz Stone, New York

CONTRACTOR / CM
Daniel O'Connell's Sons, Holyoke, MA
President
Dennis Fitzpatrick
Senior Project Manager
Alan Harwood

PERFCON CONCRETE PANELS
Beton Bolduc, Inc., Quebec
President
Yvonne Bolduc
Project Managers
Charles Theriault, Michel Martin

CLADDING AND WINDOWS
Cheviot Corporation
President
Larry Pelligrini

PHOTO CREDITS
All reasonable efforts have been made to trace the copyright holders of the visual material reproduced in this book. The publisher and the Knowlton School of Architecture apologize to anyone who has not been reached. Errors and omissions will be corrected in future editions.

All images courtesy of Steven Holl Architects except as follows:

Photos by Dan Carney
24 left, center, and right

Photos by Andy Ryan
Cover, 7 far right, 68, 77, 78, 95, 100 bottom left and far right, 103, 106, 108 left, 110, 111, 115, 117–51, 154–57

Photos by Paul Warchol
17, 112, 113

BIBLIOGRAPHY

Acerboni, Francesca. "Simmons Hall, MIT Undergraduate Residence." *Elite* 8 (August 2003): 24–35.

Amelar, Sarah. "Simmons Hall, Massachusetts." *Architectural Record* 110, no. 4 (May 2003): 204–15.

Bernstein, Fred. "Full of Holes." *Riba Journal*, April 2003, 46–56.

Campbell, Robert. "MIT's New Dorm is Extraordinary, Inside and Out." *Boston Sunday Globe*, October 20, 2002.

Dall'Olio, Lorenzo. "Residenze universitarie a Cambridge." *L'industria delle costruzioni* 369 (January–February 2003): 27–37.

Eisen, David. "Architecture; Dorm beyond the Norm; MIT's Simmons Hall is a Triumph of Modern Design for Student Living." *Boston Herald*, October 6, 2002.

"El pulmon del campus." *Ottagano* 154 (November 2002): 54–59.

Flint, Anthony. "Sense of Place; At MIT, Going Boldly Where No Architect Has Gone Before." *Boston Globe*, October 13, 2002.

Griffith, Victoria. "A Hole New Take on Design." *The Financial Times* (London), April 11, 2003.

Lieber, Jeffrey. "Simmons Hall." *Bauwelt*, April 2003, 10–15.

Pendleton, Ann. "Simmons Hall di Steven Holl." *Il Giornalle Dell'Architettura* 5 (March 2003), 22–23.

"Residenza Per Studenti, MIT—Cambridge, USA; Simmons Hall, MIT—Cambridge, USA, Steven Holl Architects." *The Plan* 4 (September 2003): 38–51.

Safran, Yehuda. "Holl's Hall of Residence for MIT is His Most Significant Building Yet." *Domus* 472 (April 2003): 40–61.

"Simmons Hall, MIT Undergraduate Residence, Cambridge, Massachusetts, USA 1999–2002" *a+u*, August 2003, 12–23.

"Simmons Hall, MIT Undergraduate Residence, Cambridge, Massachusetts, China, 2001." *World Architecture* 160 (October 2003): 24–37.

"Steven Holl, Simmons Hall, Cambridge Massachusetts, USA, Design 1999–2000, Construction 2000–2003." *GA Document* 74 (June 2003): 50–77.

"Steven Holl at MIT." *Abitare* 427 (April 2003): 242–52.

"Un campus en mutation, Simmons Hall, residence universitaire au MIT, Cambridge, USA." *Architecture Interieure*, July–August 2003, 104–11.

BIOGRAPHIES

TODD GANNON is a lecturer in architectural theory and design at the Knowlton School of Architecture and a project designer at Acock Associates Architects in Columbus, Ohio. Previous books include *Morphosis/Diamond Ranch High School*, *Bernard Tschumi/Zénith de Rouen*, *UN Studio/Erasmus Bridge*, and *The Light Construction Reader*.

MICHAEL DENISON is a graduate of the Knowlton School of Architecture and a designer with Jonathan Barnes Architecture and Design in Columbus, Ohio.

YEHUDA SAFRAN is an art and architectural critic based in Paris and New York and is currently adjunct associate professor of architecture at Columbia University. His writings have appeared in *Domus*, *Sight and Sound*, *Lotus*, *a+u*, and *AA Files*. His book *Mies van der Rohe* was published in 2000.

ANDY RYAN is a freelance photographer based in Cambridge, MA. He is currently documenting the completion of MIT's twelve-building Capital Projects and New York City's Second Avenue Subway Project. His work has appeared in numerous publications including *New York Times Magazine*, *Architectural Record*, *Archaeology*, *RIBA Journal*, *Huaser*, *Ottagono*, *Scientific American*, *Engineering News Record*, *Architecture*, *Stern*, and *Condé Nast Traveler*. His books include *The Big Dig*, *Bugialli on Pasta*, *Foods of Naples*, *The All American Cheese and Wine Book,* and the upcoming *Stair Steps to the Gods* and *Foods of Parma*, due out in 2004. His work can be viewed at www.andyryan.com.